Cambridge E[...]
....
Le[...]

D1101792

Series editor:

Dragons' Eggs

J. M. Newsome

CAMBRIDGE
UNIVERSITY PRESS

CAMBRIDGE UNIVERSITY PRESS
Cambridge, New York, Melbourne, Madrid, Cape Town, Singapore,
São Paulo, Delhi, Dubai, Tokyo

Cambridge University Press
The Edinburgh Building, Cambridge CB2 8RU, UK

www.cambridge.org
Information on this title: www.cambridge.org/9780521132640

First published 2010

J. M. Newsome has asserted her right to be identified as the Author of the Work in
accordance with the Copyright, Designs and Patents Act 1988.

Printed in China by Sheck Wah Tong Printing Press Limited

Typeset by Aptara Inc.

Map artwork by Malcolm Barnes

A catalogue record of this publication is available from the British Library.

ISBN 978-0-521-13264 0 Paperback
ISBN 978-0-521-17904 1 Paperback plus audio CD

*The author wishes to thank Kate Williams for cutting Gordian knots,
Lisa Grainger and Matthew Mbanga for cultural comments, Prem Rawat for
his wisdom, the Halo Trust, and Will Powell of CSSI Tanzania, for help with
technical information (any errors in this information are the author's own).*

Contents

Characters

Tendai Muruvi: an eighteen-year-old man living in Zimbabwe

Sibongile: a seventeen-year-old woman from Harare

Beatrice: a friend of Sibongile's

Shamba Muruvi: Tendai's father

Abigail Majozi: Shamba Muruvi's second wife and Tendai's stepmother

Amos Muruvi: Abigail's and Shamba's six-year-old son

Gugu Muruvi: Abigail's and Shamba's one-year-old daughter

Memory Muruvi: Abigail's and Shamba's eleven-year-old daughter

Chief Winston Majozi: Abigail's uncle

Aunt Ivy: Chief Winston's wife

Zola: a young woman volunteer and journalist

Nomalanga: an old woman

Mrs Ndlovu: a safari camp manager

Alfred: a safari guide

Mayor Method Kapuya: leader of the town council

Mr McInley: a hotel owner

Bart Gresham: a landmine expert

Mrs Gresham: Bart's wife

Gareth Gresham: Bart's son

Kit: a working dog

This story is set in Zimbabwe in 2006. Sikumi, Baobab Cross, Mangwe Ford and Elephant Junction are all imaginary. The other places mentioned are real.

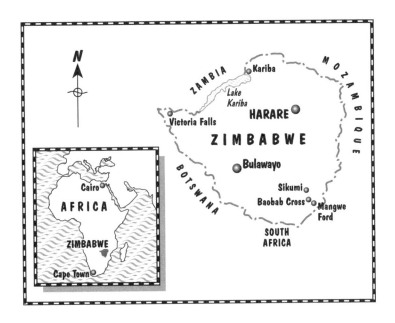

In 2007 over 5400 people (more than 14 per day) were killed or injured by landmines all over the world. Most governments do not help survivors directly. The International Red Cross and other non-governmental organisations (NGOs) and charities try to take care of survivors. Landmine clearance is also usually done by NGOs. Some of these collect their own money, some are paid by charities or governments. In 1997 many countries signed the United Nations agreement not to make or use landmines (The Ottawa Treaty), but the United States, India, China and Russia, among others, have not signed. Wikipedia and the United Nations websites can tell you more.

5

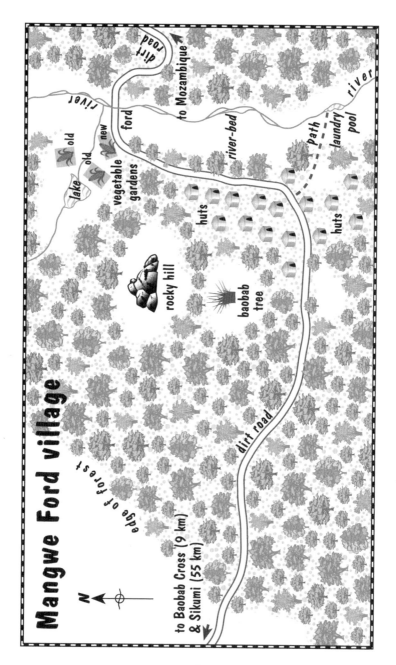

Mangwe Ford village

N

to Baobab Cross (9 km)
& Sikumi (55 km)

edge of forest

dirt road

rocky hill

baobab tree

huts

huts

path

laundry pool

river

river-bed

ford

vegetable gardens

lake

old

old

new

river

dirt road

to Mozambique

Chapter 1 *Punishment*

The day before I met Sibongile was my last day at school. I'd been at an expensive private high school in Harare, the capital of Zimbabwe, for seven years. But on the day I met Sibongile I woke up in the small village of Mangwe Ford. The houses were huts made of mud and grass, there was no electricity or running water, and the nearest telephone was two hours' walk away. I felt lost, like a train without its rails.

The sun was rising when I came out of the guest hut where I'd slept. In front of me was a clearing in the forest with huge trees all around it. Sunlight sliced between the branches. On the other side of the clearing a tall young woman with a huge basket on her head was walking away from me along a path. Dust rose round her feet. There was no one else around, but I could smell smoke from a cooking fire somewhere. My six-year-old brother Amos, who'd slept beside me on the floor, had gone out earlier.

I stepped away from the door and a second young woman, who was hurrying to catch the other one up, ran into me. Her basket went flying. T-shirts, dresses and underwear rained down as I held her arm to stop her falling over.

'I didn't see you,' she said.

'Obviously,' I replied. 'Are you OK?'

She looked up at me from under her eyelashes with a wide smile. 'I'm fine. But you're standing on my best dress.'

I stepped back. A dress had fallen on the path. It was very dirty. 'I'm sorry,' I said. 'You're going to do your laundry?'

'Yes,' she said, picking up the clothes and putting them back in the basket. 'The clothes were already dirty, but you've made them worse. Your punishment is to help us.'

'Punishment?' I said, surprised.

'Certainly. Follow me.' She lifted her basket back on to her head and set off, her body moving invitingly.

I was confused about this 'punishment'. Was it something accepted in village culture, or just her way of laughing at a new arrival? But I followed anyway, enjoying watching her from behind.

We passed under the trees, crossed a wide area of white sand and came to the river. The other young woman was already knee-deep in the water, beating clothes on the rocks. She looked at me and smiled – a polite, friendly smile. My knees went weak and I sat down rather suddenly on a rock.

The young woman I'd followed said, 'I'm Beatrice.' She waved a hand at the tall one. 'And that's Sibongile.'

I swallowed. 'Hi,' I said. What was wrong with my voice?

Sibongile said, 'Hi,' and went back to work.

Beatrice said to me, 'Here. Take my dress. Wet it and beat it on the rock, like this.'

But I sat with the dress in my hands. I hardly heard what Beatrice said because I was watching Sibongile.

'OK,' said Beatrice. 'If you don't know how to wash clothes, you'll have to tell us all about yourself.'

'Will that be my "punishment"?' I asked.

She nodded. 'What's your name?' she shot at me.

'Tendai Muruvi,' I answered.

'And how old are you?'

'Eighteen,' I said. 'I finished school yesterday.'

'Which school?'

'A private school near Harare.' Maybe Sibongile couldn't hear me. I spoke a little louder over the sounds of the river and the laundry. 'My dad's boss, Owen Woods, was rich until last week. He paid for me to go there, and wanted me to go to university.'

Beatrice spoke as she worked. 'Is your dad ... the man who is ill? What does he do?'

'Now? Nothing. He was chief mechanic on Mr Woods' orange farm near Harare. The Woods family left suddenly last week and the farm was taken over two days later.'

Beatrice and Sibongile looked at each other. I guessed they already knew about Mr Woods' farm, and all the workers being forced to leave due to the Land Reform Programme. They knew because my stepmother, Abigail, came from this village. She'd brought my sick dad and my brother and sisters here three days ago, because she had nowhere else to go.

I said, 'But you know all that already.' Sibongile didn't react. I stood up, ready to leave. My legs were OK now.

But Beatrice wasn't going to let me go. 'Why didn't you come with your family?'

'Because I was still at school when the farm was occupied,' I said. 'I came here on the bus from Harare. It took all day, and left me at Baobab Cross. I walked from there.'

Sibongile looked up. 'Do you know Harare?' she asked.

'A bit,' I answered. She really was lovely. I sat down again.

'Do you play any sports?' asked Beatrice. Sibongile looked away again, the flying drops of water from her work making shining lines of light in the sun.

'I was captain of the school rugby team,' I answered.

Beatrice smiled at me. 'Did you bring anything nice with you, like ... chocolate?' They both exploded with laughter.

I stood up. 'Ladies,' I said, 'I must see how my father is.'

'Wouldn't you like to ask us anything?' Beatrice asked.

I was suddenly full of anger. 'Lots of things,' I shouted. 'What will my family do here? Will my dad recover? How am I going to study now? How do I get out of here?'

They both looked at me in surprise. Then Sibongile came over to me, looked me in the eyes and said, 'This is quite a large village, you know, even though it's so new. We have cows, chickens and goats, and vegetable gardens. We have cool shade, and water all year round. It was built near the Wildlife Park for tourists to visit. There are no tourists now, of course, but compared to other places, we're lucky.'

Her lovely face was completely serious. She was trying to make me feel better, but I hardly heard her words. I was trying very hard not to put my arms around her and squeeze her till she couldn't breathe. I'd never felt like that before and it confused me.

Stupidly, I said, 'I didn't want to come here.'

'It's not so bad,' Sibongile said. 'When we first came, I missed my cellphone and the TV and stuff. But it gets easier.'

'How?' I asked.

She turned back to her work with a smile. 'For a start,' she said, 'we have a wind-up charger for our cellphones now. We can charge up the batteries by hand.'

'But,' said Beatrice, 'there's no signal, so they're useless anyway.'

They both laughed at this wonderful joke. I turned back towards the huts. I had to get control of myself.

'See you later?' Beatrice asked.

'Maybe,' I said and walked back across the sand.

Chapter 2 *Thieves*

My dad was still sick. He was sitting on the earth bench by the wall in the main guest hut. His skin was dry and grey, and he seemed blind, although his eyes were open. When I spoke to him, he didn't answer. My worry and anger were like dark clouds in my mind. But my excitement at meeting Sibongile was like the sun shining between them.

I went out to sit near the fire. My baby sister Gugu was sleeping in a box on the ground. My stepmother Abigail brought me tea.

'When did Dad get like this?' I asked.

'After they occupied the farm,' she replied, sitting down on a cloth on the ground. 'He went into Harare to find work. But there were hundreds of men and no jobs. He came back, went into our house and I found him like this in the kitchen.'

'I remember hearing that he did this when my mum died,' I said. 'It seems that he got better in a few days.'

Abigail shook her head. 'He just sits, looking at his feet.'

'It's been such a shock for him,' I said. 'For all of us ...'

'Your brother and sister don't seem too upset,' said Abigail with the first smile I'd seen on her face since I arrived. 'Amos has found lots of friends and Memory's already planning our new huts.' Baby Gugu began to wake up.

Two older women came and joined us by the fire. They started talking to Abigail about making a new vegetable garden, so I went back to my hut and began to unpack.

Most of my stuff was in plastic bags. I'd had to leave a lot behind, at school. They said I could collect it later. When the plastic bags were empty, I wasn't sure what to do with them. But Amos had suddenly appeared, and he knew.

'Can I have those?' he asked.

'Sure,' I said. 'What do you want them for?'

'A ball!' he laughed up at me, his teeth shining white in the dark hut.

'Of course. Want some help?' I felt myself smiling. His little round cheeks caught the light from the door. He took my hand and led me outside.

We sat on the earth with our backs against the mud wall of the hut. It was shady there, under the huge trees.

I started knotting the bags together. But my confused thoughts made me too fierce, and the plastic tore. Amos's big eyes looked up at me. I tried again.

Two more six- or seven-year-old boys came across the clearing in front of us. They stood watching me, waiting.

'How's that?' I asked Amos when I was satisfied.

'Great!' He jumped up and reached for the ball.

I stood up and kicked it out into the sunshine. Like magic, five or six more boys appeared. Amos got to the ball first and the game began.

I watched them for a moment. They were so happy, laughing and shouting.

I went back into the hut to look at what I'd brought with me. There was my school uniform, which I would never wear again, the jeans I was wearing and another pair, two or three T-shirts, and two pairs of shoes – probably as many clothes as most people who lived in the village. And I had some books, my maths things and my cellphone.

But I doubted we could afford to pay for that, even if there'd been a signal. One minute I was thinking, 'Life is trying to punish me!' and I wanted to swear or punch someone. The next minute I was smiling and remembering Sibongile's face.

'Now I know what "mixed-up" means,' I thought, laying out my clothes on my shelf with great care.

Abigail came in with baby Gugu tied on her back. She had some clean clothes in her hands.

'These are Amos's,' she said.

She went over and started arranging Amos's things on his shelf. I took Gugu's little hand between my fingers and made faces at her. She laughed.

The kids outside were making a lot of noise as they played.

Abigail turned to me. 'Uncle Winston and Aunt Ivy want us to eat with them today. I'm going now to help prepare the meal ...' As so often with Abigail, I couldn't be sure what she wanted from me. Abigail's Uncle Winston was the head of the village, Chief Majozi. I'd met him and Aunt Ivy the night before. I knew this meal would be important.

I was just going to ask her if I should go with her to help, when the noise of the football game suddenly stopped. We went out to see why. The children were all standing silently under a large tree, looking up.

I called out, 'What's wrong?'

Amos pointed up. 'A monkey stole the ball!' he shouted. He sounded so horrified that we all laughed.

Our laughter frightened the monkeys and they started towards the river, jumping through the branches. I ran after them with the others.

At the edge of the river-bed the trees stopped. The monkeys gathered together in the last branches and had a shouted discussion. The river-bed sand was so white that it hurt my eyes in the midday sun.

The children were jumping up and down, shouting at the monkeys. 'Thieves! Thieves! Give it back!'

'You'll get sick if you eat it,' Memory called to the monkeys. She was only eleven, but already behaved like a little mother.

The monkeys began to fight over the ball, their screams echoing through the forest. Finally, they threw it down on to the sand at the foot of a huge tree. All the boys ran towards it, with Amos in front. He always was the fastest runner.

I watched as Amos turned on one foot to kick the ball back – and suddenly flames and smoke shot out of the ground.

Chapter 3 *Blood*

Amos rose into the air and hung there for a moment like a broken doll. He fell back on to the sand, screaming. Something else fell further away and the smoke began to clear. The sound of the explosion and Amos's scream reached me in the same second.

I ran forward, Abigail just behind me.

Amos lay on his back, his arms waving crazily in the air. One hand was hanging loose, almost completely cut off. Half his left leg was missing. Blood shot into the air with the regular beat of his heart. It made red lines of drops on the sand and the clothes of the children. Abigail fell on her knees beside him, trying to stop the blood with her hands. I raced towards the huts to get help.

And I ran into Dad. He was running towards me! Aunt Ivy was with him. She had a piece of cloth and a short stick.

We got back to Amos. Aunt Ivy tied the cloth round his bleeding leg, put the stick through it and began turning. The blood stopped.

Meanwhile, Dad had torn a piece of cloth off his shirt. He turned to Abigail and tried to speak, but Memory was ready and handed him a strong stick. They stopped the bleeding in Amos's arm. His hand had fallen off.

Abigail took over from Aunt Ivy, who ran back to the huts. Amos had stopped screaming. He was unconscious.

In the strange silence Abigail said to Dad, 'Shamba, he needs to go to hospital.' Dad picked Amos up as if he was as light as a leaf and began running. He ran away from the river on the dirt road that led to Baobab Cross.

Abigail turned to me. 'Please, Tendai,' she said, and this time I knew what she wanted. I ran after Dad.

As I passed, Aunt Ivy rushed out of a hut with a backpack. She pushed it into my hands. 'Thanks,' I called and ran on.

I don't remember much of the journey, except thinking I was glad I'd trained so hard for the rugby team at school. I concentrated on where I was putting my feet. The road was stony in places. I'd walked it from the bus, but it had been dark and I'd been going slowly. Now it was light and we needed to run like cheetahs.

We both slowed down a bit for the steep rise halfway, but it was downhill from there. A bit later, Dad tripped and fell on to one knee. We stopped for a moment, too breathless to speak. I found a bottle of water in the backpack. Dad poured some into Amos's mouth, and we drank a little, taking turns.

I also found my cellphone. Good old Aunt Ivy! There was no signal, but the battery was still alive.

'Shall I take him for a bit?' I asked.

Dad gave Amos to me without a word.

We ran on. When we could see the group of huts that was the Baobab Cross Hotel in the distance, I thought of the phone again. I stopped and gave Amos to Dad. Drops of our sweat fell on Amos's face. Dad gently wiped them off.

I had a signal! Dad tried again to give Amos some water while I called the emergency services. In the end I got the hospital in Sikumi, the nearest town. They sent out a car to meet us.

In the car, Amos woke up. Well, he didn't exactly wake. He opened his eyes and looked straight through us. I thought that might be the end, but Dad got him to swallow some water. In less than half an hour we were at the hospital. They took Amos from us and disappeared inside with him.

Later, Dad and I sat in silence, side by side, in the waiting room. We'd been to the men's toilets and washed the blood off. No one had said whether Amos would live or die.

The nurses had taken some blood from my dad and me to put in the hospital blood bank. Amos had needed a lot of blood. And now my head felt like it was going round and round. It was like being very drunk, I suppose. A nurse had brought us tea with sugar.

As we sat, a young woman in jeans came up to us.

'Are you with the boy hurt by a landmine?' she asked.

I looked at Dad quickly. He was shaking his head very slowly so I said, 'Yes?' I made it a question.

'Hi. I'm Zola. I'm a volunteer. In my spare time I help out with an organisation that takes care of people like your boy. I just wanted to say that there may be other landmines.' Her fingers were very thin, with long nails painted pale blue. She held a notebook and a pen. 'Most landmines,' she went on, 'are in known minefields. They were mapped and marked with signs, although the signs have gone now. People are saying that a few landmines were laid without maps, by revolutionaries, and no one knows where they are. This may be helpful.' She gave me a piece of paper headed, '*What to do about landmines*'.

I folded it, put it in my jeans pocket, and said, 'Thanks.'

'There are companies that clear landmines and organisations, like the one I work with, that help people who are hurt. Their names are on that paper,' she said.

'Thanks,' I said again, and she left us.

17

I still felt strange, so I asked a passing nurse if I could have some more tea. She went off with a smile and came back with two steaming cups.

Before I could say anything, Dad spoke!

'Thanks very much,' he said to her. Same old voice, same old light in the eyes.

She smiled at him, touched his shoulder, and went back to work. She was pretty, I had to admit, but well over thirty.

'So ...' I said to Dad. 'You're OK if there's a pretty woman around, then.'

'Remember that,' he said, with the ghost of a smile. 'Next time I "go away" like that, find a beautiful woman and I'll come back, fast.'

But then he turned and looked into my face. 'What's happened to us, Tendai?' His eyes filled with tears.

We were both covered in dust and smelled of sweat. He badly needed a shave. I said, 'We've learned you can run nearly as fast as I can.' But we both knew what had happened to us. Disaster.

Dad's tears fell on to his trousers. Questions poured out of his mouth. 'What are landmines doing in that bit of the river? Will it happen again? Will Abigail keep the girls away from the river-bed? Why didn't someone warn us?'

'Perhaps it was the first time?' I said.

His questions hung in the air, mixing with the hospital smells. He took my hand, and held it in his.

We sat there looking at the wall. I remembered the tea.

'Drink up,' I said with the best smile I could manage. 'We'll need our strength for the run back.'

Finally a woman doctor came out to us. We stood up and I examined her face. She just looked tired.

Chapter 4 *Hope*

The doctor said, 'Amos will live.' Dad took a deep breath. I let my breath out. 'But he must stay here for two or three weeks,' she continued, 'and he'll need more blood. Then he'll need nursing at home for two or three months or more, while his wounds close completely.'

'Thank you, Doctor,' Dad said.

'If you agree, someone from the Landmine Injury Rescue Organisation will come and see him before he leaves here. It may be that they can get a leg made for him later. They don't make hands.'

'What do you mean?' I asked.

'The LIRO is an organisation that arranges for people who are wounded by landmines to have what are called prostheses. These are artificial arms and legs, so the wounded person can live more normally.'

I thought, 'That's what Zola with the blue fingernails must have meant.' I hadn't read what she'd given me, and I'd been thinking Amos would be a kind of vegetable for the rest of his life – if he lived.

'Anyway, he will have a crutch,' she added.

Dad hadn't been listening. He'd been trying to see into the room where Amos was. He suddenly asked, 'What's that?'

'It's a wooden stick that fits under the arm and works instead of the missing leg.'

'I didn't . . . A crutch. Of course,' he said.

'They won't be able to make him a leg until he's completely well,' she went on. 'And even then it's often difficult for children, because they're still growing.'

But Dad was smiling. 'That's wonderful,' he said. 'Thank you!' He took her hand and shook it hard.

'He's still asleep. The nurse will tell you when you can see him.' She smiled a tiny, tired smile, pulled her hand out of Dad's, and left us.

Dad put his arms around me and squeezed the breath out of me. 'Thank you too, Tendai.' He was grinning. 'Without you I wouldn't have made it and Amos would have died.'

I freed myself with a laugh. 'Well, now you'll have to pay the price. I'm dying of hunger!'

He let me go and we left the hospital to find food.

We went to an eating house and ordered chicken and rice. We sat on high little chairs in the window, looking out.

'Eating in a restaurant,' I joked. 'You a millionaire now?'

'Sure.' Dad didn't smile. 'Enjoy it. We're celebrating.'

The silence came back, thick and heavy.

When we'd had enough, we sat back with mugs of tea. Dad was looking straight ahead at the people in the street.

'Do you remember last time you were home from school?' he began.

'The winter holidays,' I put in. 'I passed my driving test.'

'Right. We had a visit from some guys in uniform?'

'Yeah, I remember. They were pretty nasty.'

'They came again three or four times.'

'So that's why the Woods family left?' I asked.

'Yes. I believe Mr and Mrs Woods finally got scared,' he said. 'They just left without telling us. They'd been on the farm for three generations … They seem to have gone to Australia … They gave us a good life for a long time.'

I couldn't bear his being so calm. I shouted at him, 'But you worked hard! And now you're left with nothing after all those years. And Memory and Amos won't get their education …'

He looked at me. 'Tendai, you have a right to be angry,' he said. 'But it doesn't solve anything. I feel powerless too. But we Zimbabweans survive because we can change as our circumstances change. And that's what we have to do now.'

'But you "went away",' I said, 'and left Abigail to deal with this on her own.'

Dad looked down again, his eyes full of tears. 'I didn't do that on purpose – and I'm back now.'

I kept quiet. I had no answer except an angry one.

After a while, Dad said, 'We have to decide how we're going to live. Abigail's Uncle Winston is offering us part of the land where they grow vegetables, and help with building some huts – our own little compound. The rains have been bad so far this year, but in Mangwe Ford they always have water. My own family lands were taken by white people a long time ago, so we have nowhere else to go.'

I took a deep breath. 'Then I suppose we'd better be grateful for the offer to live back in the Stone Age!' I said. 'Do we have any money at all? Perhaps I can get a job. I went to one of the best schools in the country, after all.'

Dad smiled, calm as a windless dawn, ignoring my angry voice and my question about money. 'Maybe you can. But I hope we can get our home in the village organised first. I need your help with that. Then you can start looking for work.'

Chapter 5   *Back to the village*

Later, during the night, we were allowed to see Amos. He was sleeping deeply, a small black boy in a huge white bed. We phoned the Baobab Cross Hotel and left a message for Abigail. It was the nearest phone to Mangwe Ford. We said that Dad would stay with Amos, and Abigail should come as soon as she could. We slept on chairs in the waiting room, and agreed they weren't as comfortable as the floor of a hut.

Then, at first light, I set off back to the village on foot.

There was a truck stop with a café and bottle store at the edge of Sikumi. One of the drivers was happy to give me a lift if I kept him awake, he said. I told him the story of the latest Will Smith film while his noisy old truck fought with the hills. It was very good to get out at Baobab Cross.

Abigail came hurrying towards me from the hotel, her skirt bright blue against the red earth.

'Is it true?' she asked. 'He'll live?'

'It's true,' I said. 'Amos will live and Dad's OK now.'

'I didn't dare believe it,' she said with a smile. 'Memory and Gugu are staying in Uncle Winston's compound. Give them a kiss from me.'

And she was gone, walking fast down the road to Sikumi.

I drank some water and took the red dirt road towards the village. I'd given my cellphone to Dad, as the nurse had said she'd charge it for him. So now I was leaving the last electricity and telephone behind.

This thought brought my anger back, and I began to

run. I kept my mind busy, making lists of all the bad things that had happened to us, all the bad things that still might happen to us, and what I would do to the people who'd made them happen. That got me about halfway.

I slowed to a walk. 'Now think about something nice,' I told myself. So I thought about Sibongile, and the shining drops of water falling round her as she worked, making her T-shirt stick to her skin as they fell on her. I wondered what she'd meant by saying, 'When we first came …' Where had she come from, and who were 'we'? And how did she make me feel the way she did? She obviously wasn't trying to.

I looked up at the clear blue sky – no sign of rain – and saw two great birds circling. All around me were small trees, with wide areas of rocky red earth between them. In the distance I could see zebra eating tired green grass. Suddenly they began to run. They crossed the road ahead of me, leaving a cloud of dust. Maybe something big was hunting. These hills were home to a lot more animals than people. I began to run again, too. But when I got to the top of the rise, I stopped to look at the view.

Four or five kilometres away, thick forest grew on either side of the wide sandy river-bed. The river itself was a thin line of rocks and water near the far side. The dirt road wound down and was lost in the forest in front of me. I could see where it crossed the river at the ford, a shallow place with no rocks. It went into the trees on the far bank, and came out above them on to low, empty hills. From there I knew the border with Mozambique was a day's walk away.

I hurried on to the village, looking forward to a wash and clean clothes – and to seeing Sibongile again, even from a distance.

Later, I went to Uncle Winston's compound. I could hear Aunt Ivy singing in her cooking hut.

'Knock, knock,' I called.

She came out calling, 'Memory! Your brother's back ... Come in, Tendai, come in.'

Memory sat with me while I ate Aunt Ivy's biscuits and fruit and told her about the hospital. Gugu played outside with some baby chickens. After a few minutes, Uncle Winston came in. He was a tall man with an almost Arab face, wearing jeans and a purple Nelson Mandela-style shirt.

'We've never had a landmine in this village before,' he told me. 'Thank goodness Ivy knew what to do.'

I said, ' Yes, Amos could have died without your help.'

Aunt Ivy said, 'Stop your nonsense.'

When I'd finished eating, Uncle Winston asked me if I was free. I stood up immediately.

'Come with me,' he said. 'I need your help.'

We went to his private hut, where there was a desk and bookshelves. On the desk was a letter. There were a lot of corrections on it.

'I'm writing to the mayor,' he said, 'to ask what he's doing about the landmines. We've asked many times for the minefield across the river to be cleared. There was talk of starting some months ago. And now we know there are landmines near the village. I want you to check this letter over for mistakes in the English.' Uncle Winston pulled up a chair for me.

I checked through the letter and found it almost perfect. Just as I finished, a shadow filled the doorway.

Chapter 6 *Sibongile*

'Ah,' said Uncle Winston. 'Come in, dear Sibongile. Tendai has given me his opinion. Now you can tell me yours.'

I didn't hear Sibongile's reply because my heart had started beating too loudly. I stood up to let her sit down at the desk and I had to hold on to the chair. I'd thought the feeling would get less as I saw more of her, but it was worse.

I took a couple of deep breaths, wondering whether she felt it too, but she didn't seem to. When she'd finished, Uncle Winston almost pushed us out of the door together.

I walked to the gate and held it open for her. I was in control again now. I tried to look cool, but I felt like I was flying. We walked towards her hut together.

'How's Amos?' she asked.

'He'll be OK.' Trying to look cool wasn't working. Even Amos's terrible problems couldn't stop me smiling. 'He'll just need a new leg and to learn to write with his left hand.' I suddenly thought, 'This feeling is called happiness!'

'That's all, is it?' she asked with her head on one side. She was laughing at me a little.

We'd stopped outside her hut. She called to someone inside, 'Do you hear that, Useni? Be careful where you walk if you want to grow up with two legs.'

A boy of about twelve came out of the hut. He blew down his nose. 'Pphh. This place is disgusting!'

'Don't be rude, Useni,' Sibongile said, embarrassed. 'Tendai, this is Useni, my brother. Useni, if we weren't here we'd have to live at Grandma's, where there's no water. Here is better.'

Useni took a last swallow from his can of cola and threw it on the ground. 'Why did Mum have to die, anyway?' he shouted. 'And why won't they let us see Dad?'

'Useni,' said Sibongile, pointing to the can.

'Let's go and see the guys playing football,' I said.

Useni looked a bit happier at that, picked up the can and set off across the clearing. A match had started near the road to Baobab Cross. His sister and I followed more slowly.

Sibongile means 'thankful'. So I said, 'You have a lovely name.' But as soon as I'd said it, I felt stupid.

I felt better though when she said 'thank you' quietly.

'I was wondering,' I said, 'how long you've been here.'

'We've visited many times,' she said. 'But we came about a week ago to stay, maybe for ever.'

'Where were you living before, then?' I asked.

'In Harare,' she answered. 'Our mother died some time ago ... And now our father is in hospital, also dying.' She didn't sound particularly upset about her dad, I thought. 'And his father insisted we came here now, so Useni can start at the church school near Baobab Cross in the New Year.'

'But surely you could have stayed in Harare and lived there with your grandfather?' I asked.

'But he doesn't live there,' replied Sibongile. 'He lives here, in Mangwe Ford. He's related to Uncle Winston, like most of us here!'

'And what about your own education?' I asked.

Just then, Aunt Ivy called from behind us and we turned.

'I have to go,' Sibongile said, 'but I have lots of questions I wanted to ask you.'

'Not as punishment for anything, I hope,' I said.

She laughed and waved as she ran back to Uncle Winston's compound. Was it me or Harare she was interested in?

I followed Useni and watched the boys playing, but somehow my eyes didn't see them. All I could think about was Sibongile's lovely face.

I couldn't stand still, so I walked back past the huts to the vegetable gardens. I found a small lake filled by a stream running down to the main river. From the lake there were narrow paths to the gardens. These were inside high fences. There were rows and rows of onions, cabbages, and so on.

I walked on along the main path. It was the continuation of the road from Baobab Cross that ran through the village. I'd seen it from the rise on my way back from the hospital. It was wide enough to drive a car along, but there were no tyre marks. Where the road turned across the sandy river-bed towards the ford, there was a new garden marked out beside it. I thought, 'This is where Abigail and Sibongile will work.'

And that made me wonder whether there was work I could do in the village. To start with there would be our compound to build, with its huts and the fence all round. I'd been planning to get a job in Sikumi when that was finished. But now, with Sibongile in Mangwe Ford, that didn't seem such a good idea.

However, it wasn't that easy to get to see her. Aunt Ivy seemed to keep her busy all the time. I didn't see her that evening, except from a distance.

The next day Uncle Winston asked me to start work on our compound. I went a long way down the river with two other men to find tall, straight young trees to cut for the 'bones' of the huts. We got back in the evening, and Sibongile, Useni, my sisters and I all ate at Aunt Ivy's table.

Useni was feeling better. He liked singing the latest pop songs, and the village boys thought this was brilliant. After the meal there was quite a party with everyone singing and dancing. But girls danced with girls, and boys with boys. So it was only later, when everyone was going to bed, that I had a few minutes alone with Sibongile.

I walked with her to her hut. It was completely dark except for the faint starlight on the river sand, pale between the trees. My whole body felt painfully alive from the music and the excitement of being close to her again.

'You don't sing, do you?' she asked.

I laughed. 'You mean, I can't sing. I sound awful.'

'But you have a beautiful speaking voice.' Was she making fun of me?

'I used to tell traditional stories,' I told her. 'When my grandmother, my mother's mother, died, I told her stories to my friends. It was a way of keeping her near.'

'Your mother died?' asked Sibongile.

'When I was born,' I said. 'So my grandmother was like my mother . . . until she died too.' My chest felt tight.

Sibongile's hand found mine and squeezed it in the darkness. 'You should tell those stories again.' She laughed, lifting our mood. 'In the evenings, before the meal.'

'But they're for little children,' I said, holding her hand in both mine.

'Make up some new ones!' she said. 'Or change some of the old ones.'

'I'll think about it,' I said. I didn't want to say goodnight.

Sibongile pulled her hand away. 'Goodnight,' she said quietly. 'Sleep tight.'

Chapter 7 *Kisses*

Next day, late in the afternoon, I took the wood I'd cut to the place where our compound would be. Then I began looking for Sibongile. Was she avoiding me? I saw Beatrice, who told me Sibongile was busy. 'There are other people in this village apart from her, you know,' she laughed.

I'd started having ideas for a story. I decided to find a quiet place to work on it, so I went to sit on the rocks at the top of a small hill just west of the village.

The sun was going down when I heard a sound behind me. Someone was climbing up the hill towards me. I thought it was Memory, come to call me in for the evening meal, but it was Sibongile!

I stood up slowly, trying to be very cool. 'Hi,' I said.

'Hi,' she replied. She looked around and sat down carefully on the ground, her back against the warm rock.

I sat down beside her, not too near. I couldn't think of anything to say. My mind was too full – or too empty.

'Your dad's a good man,' she said at last.

'He's ... well, not the perfect dad, but pretty good,' I said.

'And your stepmother is a bit stressed out, but nice.'

'She's fine. She's been very good to me,' I said.

She spoke thoughtfully, as though she was talking about a character in a film. 'My father's a terrible man. He had AIDS and didn't tell my mother. He gave it to a friend of mine too.'

I was shocked. 'A friend of yours?' I asked.

'Yes. He tricked my best friend into his bed ...' She turned to me and said very quietly, 'She's dead now. And he beat me when I tried to ask him about it.'

I said 'But you're only a child. I mean ...'

She smiled sadly. 'I'm seventeen now. I was fifteen then ...' I didn't know what to say.

She continued, 'And now he's dying too. Stupid, isn't it?'

I nodded, my eyes on the deep-pink clouds.

She put a hand on my arm and said, 'I just wanted you to know the kind of family I come from. You're ... so sweet ...'

I almost exploded. That was not how I wanted her to think of me!

She went on, '... so sweet, and I think you don't know much about the dirty side of life.'

I felt shaken. 'I can't believe ...' I said. 'You seem to come from a wealthy home, you seem so ...'

'Money isn't everything,' she said. 'Everyone is given a body, and a brain, and a life. But what we do with our lives is what we give to ourselves – our present to ourselves.' She paused, and then went on. 'My father has given himself the present of a horrible death.'

What could I say to that? I had to change the subject, so I said, 'I'm working on a story for the kids. About landmines. This village didn't have a problem with them before, did it?'

Sibongile turned to me and laughed – such perfect teeth! 'Ah ha. So you will tell us a story,' she said.

'Perhaps,' I replied.

'Well, there is a minefield,' she began, becoming serious. 'It's a few kilometres away, across the river. It used to be marked. But people used the metal signs for other things years ago, before this village moved here.'

'So the landmines are from the war,' I said. 'Thirty years ago?'

'I suppose so,' she answered.

'At the hospital,' I said, 'there was a woman who told us there might be other landmines in our area.'

Sibongile's shoulders were tight, her face angry, her eyes half closed against the setting sun. 'That's another stupid thing people do. Wars ... Totally and incredibly stupid.' She was far angrier about that than about her father.

Then her voice changed and she turned to me. 'But, you know, we could do something about that minefield. We could get people together and demand that the landmines are cleared.'

Her eyes shone and I felt excited by her energy. I said, 'The woman at the hospital gave me a list of names and addresses. We could go into Sikumi and email them.' I'd taken the paper out of my pocket and left it in the hut.

'Yes! And we'll go with Uncle Winston to see the mayor.' She stood up and clapped her hands. 'We can put out a message on the Internet, asking for money and help. We'll make sure everyone hears about Amos. We must do something quickly.'

I stood and took her shoulders in my hands. 'You can write down what we're going to say and we'll go to the Internet café near the hospital.'

She looked at me with such an excited expression on her face that I was kissing her on the mouth before I realised what I was doing.

A storm of feeling went through my body! I had to stop kissing her so that I didn't fall down. I looked at her face. She looked shocked for a moment, and then smiled a gentle smile – not a 'come on' smile, just a friendly, happy smile. Maybe she was ignoring the storm, or maybe she was better at dealing with it than I was.

She said, just a little breathlessly, 'I ... we ... need to talk to people and plan things.'

We stood completely still in the last of the sunlight. 'Yes,' I said. 'We need to think things through.'

She looked up at me. 'Why didn't the people who laid those landmines think? Didn't they see what a danger they would be to innocent people after the war?' She turned as if to go back down to the village.

I was afraid she would rush straight off to start her campaign – and I had other plans. I kept a hand on her shoulder and said, 'Thinking is not everyone's strong point.' I turned her towards me again, held her face between my hands and kissed her, very gently. I was afraid my legs would give way if my body reacted like before.

After a moment, she drew away a little, with a sweet smile. 'No,' she agreed. 'Too many people do things because of how they feel rather than what they think.' She was making fun of me, of course. But she wasn't stopping me.

I licked my lips. They were so hot they dried immediately. I said, 'True ... But some people decide to follow their feelings rather than their thoughts. That's the difference.' I leant towards her again.

She grinned at me and said, 'Are you thinking when we kiss?'

That made me laugh, and she laughed too. I sat down again and answered seriously, looking up at her. 'Mostly, when we were kissing, I was feeling. I was feeling so happy, I couldn't think.'

To my surprise she sat down and said, 'Good, me too.'

So she really did like me! We laughed and kissed a bit more. I said, 'But that doesn't mean I couldn't think if I had to, just that I don't want to.' She kissed me back, just a little.

After a few moments she said, 'I'm beginning to think . . .'

I made myself sound cool and lazy. 'Oh no,' I said. 'That's bad. Stop now!'

She said, her lips moving against mine, 'It's getting stronger and stronger, this thought . . .'

'No, no,' I said in the same position. 'Just feel . . .'

A second or two later, she said, 'It's not going away . . .'

I leant back. 'I suppose you want me to ask what it is?'

She smiled. 'Yes,' she said and kissed my cheek.

'OK,' I said. 'What are you thinking about so much that it stops you kissing me properly? Landmine campaigns? What kind of cabbages to grow?'

Her laugh was like church bells. 'I'm thinking . . . that we must go back now. If we don't, we won't get any dinner!'

Of course I didn't want to, but it was better to stop. So I jumped up and said, 'So . . . kissing doesn't fill your hungry little stomach!' I took her hand and pulled her up.

'No,' she said, making a funny little face. 'It's a pity, but it doesn't.'

The sun had gone. We ran down the hillside in the gathering dark, trying to trip each other up.

From then on, I thought about Sibongile so much, it felt as if she was living inside me. But I didn't see much of her and we were both too busy to do anything about the landmines.

And even three days later there was still no answer to Uncle Winston's letter.

Chapter 8 *Dragons' eggs*

Then my dad came back from the hospital. He was almost his old self, laughing and telling bad jokes. Being a mechanic, he took over the building work, but kindly kept me on as his assistant. He said Amos was eating well, demanding chocolate and TV, but sometimes had bad dreams at night.

Abigail would stay with Amos till he could come home. The church she belonged to was paying for his treatment and a place for her to stay in Sikumi. In general, though, Dad was a bit mysterious about money, and I couldn't get him to tell me whether we had any or not.

The story went round that the landmine that hurt Amos had been washed down the river by floods. I wasn't sure this was true, but it made us all think carefully about where we walked, and it helped me finish making up my story. The only ones who forgot to be careful were the little kids, of course. So I made my story especially for them.

When it was ready, I told Amos's friends I'd be at the village baobab tree at sunset, and there'd be a story.

Late that afternoon I went and sat with my back against the huge tree. There were a few clouds, but still no rain. The sun seemed to be taking a rest on a hill before it disappeared completely, and the clouds flamed pink and orange. I hoped Sibongile would come to the storytelling. I wanted her to see and hear me perform. I shut my eyes and listened.

I heard children gathering quietly around me. I heard large birds making a loud fuss as they settled in the forest for the night. I heard monkeys calling far away. I smelled food cooking by the huts. Someone gave a little cough.

I opened my eyes and looked at the children. They held their breath, eyes wide open, biting their lips, waiting. Their skin shone like dark metal in the orange sunlight, and the dust hung round them, golden in the still air.

I took a deep breath. 'Long ago . . .' I began slowly.

The children all broke into wide, white smiles, making themselves comfortable and preparing to listen. The sun sank suddenly behind the hill, and the shadows disappeared.

'Long ago,' I repeated, 'when the world was young, high in the mountains, a boy called River was born. He was strong and dark, and he laughed and sang, as he ran and jumped down the mountains.'

'What did he sing?' asked a little girl called Fortune.

'He sang, "You can't catch me,"' I answered.

The children began to sing, 'You can't catch me,' and two of the larger boys began to jump about like River. Memory arrived with Useni and Sibongile, and sat down at the back of my audience. I waited until everyone was quiet.

'On his way,' I went on, 'River met a beautiful girl, called Stream. They put their arms around each other and, smiling and whispering, they joined together and travelled on between the hills . . .' I looked at Sibongile. She was looking at me thoughtfully.

Some of the children whispered together and put their arms around each other. 'Later,' I said, 'they came to a wide, flat place called a plain. Around the edges of the plain were mountains and hills. As they travelled across the plain, River and Stream gave birth to lots of children.

'These little Rivers ran along, sometimes beside their parents and sometimes near the mountains. Some went down holes to water the earth. The whole River family helped people and animals, trees and grass to grow and enjoy life.'

I lowered my voice. 'But ... while River and Stream and all the little Rivers were having such a good time, someone else, who lived under the earth of the plain, was getting more and more unhappy.'

'Who was that?' someone whispered.

'That was ... Dragon!' I answered, raising my voice.

'What's Dragon?' asked Thembi, Fortune's tiny sister, her eyes wide and white.

'Dragon has a head like a huge horse,' I answered, showing with my arms how tall the dragon was.

'And wings,' added Memory, stretching her arms out. 'And a huge long tail.'

'And in its big red stomach it makes ... FIRE,' I said, sitting forward to scare the little ones, 'which it breathes out of its mouth, whoosh.' I showed them with my hands how the flames shot out of Dragon's mouth.

The children cried out. 'Eh, eh, eh!'

'And Dragon was unhappy,' I went on. 'Once, there had been hundreds of Dragons living under the earth. They used to breathe through holes, and fire would jump out on to the plain. It burned everything for miles around. But now so many of River's children ran into the holes in the earth that the Dragons were always wet. And when they were wet, the fire in their stomachs went out, and they died. At last there were only two Dragons left.'

'A mummy Dragon and a daddy Dragon?' asked Fortune.

'That's right,' I answered. 'And Mummy and Daddy Dragon were very scared and very angry. They knew that if they didn't do something they would die and there would be no more Dragons.

'So they decided to lay lots of Dragons' eggs. The eggs would break open and hatch into little Dragons, and the Rivers would not be able to put out their fires.'

'So little Dragons can breathe fire?' asked a small boy, his teeth and eyes shining in the growing dark.

'Oh yes,' I answered. 'Their fire is very hot. The Dragons hid their eggs under the earth, sometimes in big groups, sometimes one at a time. They hoped that, if all the baby Dragons hatched together, maybe the Rivers would be dried up in the heat of their fires.'

I could hardly see the children's faces now in the growing dark. But I could feel them holding their breath.

'And did they kill the Rivers?' asked a small voice.

'No, they didn't. You know that the Rivers still run. As it turned out, the Dragon babies did not all hatch at once. Some of them are still waiting, in their eggs, under the earth.'

'Is that what hurt Amos?' a boy asked.

'Yes,' I replied. 'A Dragon's egg hatched and hurt him.'

'How do you know?' asked another boy's voice in the darkness.

'You saw it happen,' I said. 'The eggs only hatch if people or animals step on them.' I raised my voice. 'And then … they JUMP out of the earth with a bang! And they bite and burn! Sometimes they bite off a leg or an arm – or both, like Amos! And sometimes they are strong enough to kill.'

'So it's a Dragon's egg that bit Amos, is it?' That was Useni's voice, deeply disbelieving.

I took no notice. 'And the Dragons laid a lot of eggs near our river and in the hills on the other side. So you must be very careful where you play. Listen to your parents when they tell you not to go somewhere.'

'Do they know where the Dragons left their eggs?'

'They know some of the places. But the Dragons hid so many eggs, no one knows where they all are. So you should stay where you know it's safe.'

The children were silent for a few seconds while the night noises grew around us. Even Useni didn't speak.

A sudden sound from the huts made everyone jump. Fortune's mother was banging a spoon on a saucepan and calling, 'Food's ready!'

The children jumped up, laughing and shouting, and ran towards the cooking fires. 'Mind the Dragons' eggs,' I called as I stood up and stretched.

Sibongile fell into step beside me as we walked towards the firelight. Her hand touched mine and held it for a few moments in the darkness. She stopped to look at the remaining light in the sky. A thin new moon had risen. I turned her towards me for a kiss, but she pulled gently away.

'You know,' she said, 'Uncle Winston likes our being together, but Aunt Ivy and the older women are giving me a hard time. That's why I'm being a bit ...'

'Keeping a safe distance?' I asked.

'I suppose that's what they want.' She laughed.

'Just one kiss?' I begged.

I got my kiss, but only the one. Then we hurried down to join everyone for the evening meal.

Chapter 9   *Lost*

The children told their parents how much they liked my story while we ate. And Useni even sang a rap about Dragons' eggs. So the next morning I was feeling on top of the world.

Sibongile came up to me as I was setting off with Dad to cut the last of our fence posts. She was wearing tight jeans and blue and white trainers. She looked so perfect I could hardly breathe. Dad made a 'wow' face and walked on ahead.

'I didn't tell you how much I liked your story,' she said. I could see that her heart was beating fast.

'Thank you,' I managed to say.

'You'll be starting to build the fence today,' she said, 'now that you've got all the wood together.'

'Probably,' I said.

'I'll be working in the new garden,' she said, 'but I should be finished before dark.'

She was asking me for a date! My heart thundered in my ears. 'Shall we meet at the rocks on the hill again,' I asked, 'to watch the sun go down?'

'That would be nice,' she said.

'Yes, it would,' I agreed.

'No story tonight?' she asked, with a smile.

'Not before supper,' I answered, grinning. 'Maybe round the fire later.'

'Do you have more stories?' she said as we walked slowly after Dad.

'There are a million stories. It's a long time since I told any, though. There wasn't much interest in them at school!' We laughed.

'No, there wouldn't be,' she said. 'There's TV and movies and Internet in the cities. Here, though, it seems right to tell stories ...' She stopped, and turned to me. 'I really like it here. But I know it's not your favourite place.'

I looked into her eyes. 'We can talk about that this evening,' I said.

'And about getting in touch with the people on the list you got from the hospital.' She smiled and turned back towards the village gardens.

Those were the happiest minutes of my life.

* * *

Later that morning Dad and I were finishing part of the fence, when we heard that terrible noise again. BANG!

A cloud of black smoke was rising, and we ran towards it. It was near the fenced gardens, where the road turned to cross the river. Everyone from the village was running that way. When we got there, I was at the front. There was a terrible smell of burning, and the smoke was blowing away.

The new garden had been cleared of all the trees and bushes. Half of it had been worked on and was ready to plant. There was a deep hole in the line where the work had stopped. The rest was still smooth, hard earth. On that earth was a woman, lying on the ground with two others kneeling beside her, their hands covering their faces.

The woman had no head and, as I got nearer, I saw she had no arms either. There was a lot of blood, but I could still see her blue and white trainers.

As I ran to the edge of the clearing to be sick, I saw Sibongile's face looking up at me from the tall grass. It was just her head, there in the grass, the eyes open in surprise, the perfect teeth showing a little between her lips.

I stood there, screaming, staring at her. I felt hands pull me away and I shut my eyes, but I could still see her.

Then I shook off the hands and ran.

* * *

I don't remember much of the next few days, but I ran a long way, and Sibongile's face was always there when I shut my eyes. Her gentle voice filled my head as I ran. '*I really like it here*,' she kept saying.

At one point in the dark, I climbed into a tree. There were monkeys sleeping there, but they kept away from me. Later, I sat among some rocks on a hilltop as daylight began. A family of rock rabbits lived there and they smelled awful. A small deer jumped up the rocks as the sun came up. It looked around, then jumped back down. It didn't see me.

Another time I drank bitter water from a pool in the rock. It didn't taste good, but I didn't care.

I remember standing on an old ants' nest and seeing thousands of deer and zebra. And later, at a big waterhole full of green plants and birds, I was surprised by a buffalo.

I was sick, and covered it with sand using a stick.

I remember a tree with yellow fruit, which was sweet and good. And there was another tree that I climbed up into and ate nuts. I threw the shells down and annoyed some birds that ran about like chickens. My tears fell all the way to the ground and made little holes in the dust.

I could feel Sibongile with me all the time. She sometimes said, '*We must go*', or '*Be careful where you walk*'. And every time I closed my eyes she was looking at me, her mouth partly open, grass in her hair.

*　*　*

A long time later I sat on a rock by a wide path made by the great, flat feet of elephants. And, when the sky was yellow and pink, they walked by. The largest one almost touched me with her long trunk, but walked on. The little ones had to run to keep up. Something made me follow them.

They came to a river, quite a small one. They walked into the water and began rolling around, drinking and washing. I went further up and found a place where the water was cleaner. I drank and washed.

I sat on rocks still warm from the sun, eating some fruit and listening to the elephants finishing their bath. I realised I was still crying.

Closing my eyes still seemed impossible, but I must have slept a bit. When day came and I went down to the water to wash my salty face, I saw the footprints of a large cat. They were as big as my hand. Perhaps my crying had frightened it away. Or perhaps it hadn't liked my smell.

That was when I understood I was lost.

I must have entered the Wildlife Park. It's huge, of course, with very few villages and hundreds of square kilometres of empty land, except for the animals.

Fear rushed into me, and I began to shake all over. I looked around, and every bush seemed to hide a lion.

I knew then that I should think about going back to the village and my family. But which way was back?

Chapter 10   *Found*

It was terrifying to have my power of thought come back. It came in little waves. That first one, when I realised I was lost, was the worst. My body didn't stop shaking all that day.

I thought I'd better follow the river. Rivers attract all kinds of animals and I might find food more easily there. Later I realised that being near the river also meant I might become food more easily.

I remember lying looking up at the stars, listening to the night – a leopard coughing, the river running over rocks, the insects getting quieter as they cooled down. The stars were like liquid diamonds, millions of them. I wondered how it would feel if they began to fall on me. For the first time in days I realised Sibongile's voice was quiet and I wasn't crying. That made me cry again.

*   *   *

At dawn – I think it was the next day – I came to a place where the river made a waterfall. I climbed down, but fell the last bit into deep water. I swam to the edge, thinking of crocodiles.

As I was getting out of the water, I thought I heard a human voice shout above the sound of the waterfall.

I looked around. The trees were quite small here, and there were rocks everywhere. I couldn't see anyone.

I emptied out my shoes and set off, following the river again. Not far on, I had to make my way through traffic jams of deer getting their morning drink.

The river soon became quite wide, full of sandy islands. I knew crocodiles loved lying on the sand, so I stayed back from the water, under the trees.

I had crossed the tyre marks in the deep sand before I realised what they were. I ran back and looked at them carefully. They came down to the river, turned in a big circle and returned. They were wide, perhaps from a small truck, but they looked quite old, the edges breaking down. They climbed a little rise and disappeared. For some strange reason, I decided not to follow them and turned back to the river.

'Eh! Where are you going?'

So it was a human voice. I stood still, looking round. An old woman, black against the sky at the top of the little rise, was leaning on a stick.

'I'm looking for Mangwe Ford,' I answered. My voice didn't work very well.

'Don't know it,' she said, and laughed like a machine gun.

'Where are you from?' I asked, afraid she'd disappear.

'Come up here,' she called.

I climbed up to her and saw miles of empty brown land with a few dusty trees, a giraffe or two and some rocky hills in the distance. The old woman stood beside me, smelling me. Her head was lower than my shoulders, so I was a bit embarrassed by that.

She said, 'You're not sick, but you're hungry.' She set off walking fast across the empty land, beside the tyre marks.

I tried to follow, but she walked so fast I got left behind. She came back to me and produced a plastic bottle of water. The water was warm, but so sweet! I hadn't drunk clean water in – how many days?

'Come on,' she said. 'It's getting too hot.'

'How far are we going?' I asked.

'To my place,' she said.

'Very helpful,' I thought, half running, half walking to keep up with her.

At last we came to a large group of tall trees and bushes. As we approached, she made a high calling sound. A small boy appeared from between the bushes. We followed him through into a clear space. There were three beautiful huts built under the trees. They were perfectly round, with highly decorated walls, and patterns cut into the grass roofs.

'We're a tourist attraction,' the old woman said, with her machine-gun laugh. 'Tuesday, Friday and Sunday mornings.'

There was a fat black pot on an open fire. It was steaming and smelled wonderful. I almost fainted as the hunger washed through me, and I had to sit down on the ground. The boy brought me a metal plate of meat in sauce and a piece of bread. The plate was too hot to hold, so he put it on the ground in front of me. The old woman brought me water in a bowl and a small, expensive towel to wash my hands.

I ate, using my fingers. I forgot to go slowly, and had to stop for a few minutes, my stomach hurt so much.

'You've been lost a long time,' she said.

'Just a few days,' I said.

'And you were in Mangwe Ford?' she asked.

'Yes,' I said. 'Is it far?'

'Don't know, but the boss at Main Camp has maps,' she replied.

'So this is part of a safari place?' I asked.

'They come straight from the airport with their cameras.' She pointed at my plate. 'More?'

'I can't just now,' I said. I could feel my body shutting down. 'I need to sleep now. I'm sorry.'

'This way,' she said, grabbing my hand and pulling me up. She led me over to one of the colourful huts. Inside was a bed with a grass mattress – a bit different from my blankets on the floor in the village. I don't even remember lying down.

When I woke it was dark. I could hear someone breathing heavily in one of the other huts, and was that a lion in the distance? I remembered where I was, and why. I tried to think about the elephants in the water and the sweet yellow fruit, but Sibongile's shoes and the screams of the women wouldn't leave me. '*It's not going away,*' Sibongile said.

Chapter 11 *Stars*

Suddenly it was day. The old woman stood over my bed. 'Tell me what happened before I talk to the boss,' she said.

'OK,' I said, half asleep.

She showed me the toilet hut and the washing place and went to make breakfast. I joined her and we sat on the ground in silence, drinking tea. After a while I asked where the little boy was, and she said, 'School.'

'I'm called Tendai,' I said. 'What should I call you?'

'My name is Nomalanga, but you can call me Gogo. Are you ready to talk?' she asked.

I didn't answer. Gogo was what I'd called my grandmother. Nomalanga took me by the hand and we went and sat under a huge spreading tree. She laid a coloured cloth down on the ground and we sat on it, a little apart.

'Begin,' she said.

I began with the family leaving the farm. I told her about the way Dad had 'gone away' and the village. Then I went back and told her about school, about my friends.

'Good,' she said. She got up and brought water and dried fruit. 'Now, tell me why you ran away.'

I thought, 'Maybe she thinks I'm a criminal.' I told her about Amos and the hospital. But then I was quiet. I could hear Sibongile's voice in my head. She said, '*But you know, we could do something about that minefield,*' again and again. I kept trying to tell Nomalanga about her, but I couldn't. I just saw her head in the grass again, and the blue and white trainers. I began to shake. Nomalanga got up and left me there. I think I slept.

When I opened my eyes again she was back.

'Mangwe Ford is eighty kilometres away, near the border,' she said. I could see the respect in her eyes.

'Wow,' I said.

'Food?' she asked.

'Thank you, Gogo. Yes, please.'

It was getting towards sunset. We didn't talk much while we ate. I helped wash the plates.

Then she took my hand again and led me to a place beyond the trees. She sat on her cloth and leaned back against a huge rock. I sat down beside her. 'Look,' she said, and waved her hand at the view.

There was a large waterhole below us, a splash of green in the red and brown landscape. Hundreds of birds were there, tall slim ones fishing, and smaller rounder ones swimming. There was a pair of crazy ones, flying up and rolling and falling out of the sky, their bright blue wings flashing.

Nomalanga smoothed the back of my hand with her rough fingers. 'You must talk to me,' she said. 'You must talk so you can sleep without dreams, live without voices.'

As I looked out over the waterhole, the sky filled with tiny birds. They made moving patterns as they prepared to settle for the night. 'I didn't have dreams last night,' I said.

'Hm hmm!' She laughed gently. 'You called names in your sleep after you'd spent a long time crying.'

'How can you know that?' I asked. 'You were asleep in your hut.'

'Not all night,' she replied calmly. She didn't say any more but kept hold of my hand.

I watched the little birds, like smoke against the orange sky. They made a sound like wind in the grass. I forced myself to speak. 'Her name was ... Sibongile,' I said.

As I talked, and remembered, and talked some more, the tears came again. And I held on to Nomalanga's hand as though she could stop me from drowning in them. When I told her about the Dragons' eggs story I'd told the children, just the day before Sibongile was killed, she held my face between her hands and said, 'No, dear boy, you are not guilty. It was not your doing.'

It was dark when I finished. The birds were silent, the insects quiet. Nomalanga didn't speak for a while. Then she said, 'You have loved and been loved. That is a great gift.' She paused. 'Sibongile died so quickly she didn't feel fear or pain. That is also a gift.' She held my hand tight for a moment. 'There are those who love by holding on ...' Then she put my hand down on my leg and left it there. 'And there are those who love by letting go. It's your decision.'

I couldn't speak, but my heart felt lighter. I heard Sibongile in my head say, '*You're so sweet ...*'. I felt a small smile on my lips. She wasn't letting go of me just yet, and I was glad.

Nomalanga took a breath and blew out through her nose.

'Ppph. Tomorrow's Tuesday,' she said. 'The tourists will be here a couple of hours after sunrise.' She stood up and pulled me up too. 'You can get a lift with them to Main Camp. Then you can ask the boss about getting home.'

We walked back to the huts in the starlight.

'I want to thank you, Gogo,' I said. 'How can I do that?'

'You say you tell stories?' I could hear she was smiling in the dark.

'Yes, I do, but I would be shy to tell a lady such as you any of my stories.'

'Then you can be polite and drink a beer with me and listen while I tell you one.'

Something moved in the darkness near me, making me jump. A young voice said, 'Can we listen, too, Gogo?'

'Hmm,' said Nomalanga, placing her little wooden seat carefully. I could just see five children as they sat on the sandy earth in a half-circle. I thought, 'Where did they all come from?' She handed me a bottle of beer. I sat with the children on the ground. She spent a long time lighting a pipe. The smoke rose, pale as a ghost in the starlight.

'Long ago, when the Lion was King,' she began in the sing-song voice of the traditional storyteller, 'there were no stars and the nights were completely dark.' The children and I all looked up at the shining beauty of the sky, trying to imagine complete darkness. 'This made King Lion's life difficult,' she went on. 'During the day the sun was too hot for him to run and hunt. And during the night he couldn't see unless there was a moon. And many times, as you know, there wouldn't be one, so he would go hungry for days on end.

'Once, when he hadn't eaten for some days, he found a group of humans living in a hole in the rocks. Humans were dangerous, so he waited until one of the children came out alone. Then he grabbed it and held it in his mouth.

'The little Boy – for it was a boy, not a girl, thank goodness …' The children laughed and the boys clapped. 'The Boy,' she went on, 'had his catapult with him. And before King Lion could eat him, he shouted, "Don't try to eat me. I'm very strong and I have my catapult and my bag of stones. I shall make holes in your stomach and you will die."'

One of the boys jumped up. 'I've got a catapult,' he cried, taking a Y-shaped stick from his pocket and making the movements of shooting at birds with it. The other children pulled him down. Nomalanga ignored him.

She said, 'King Lion was surprised and put the Boy down. "But I'm very hungry," he said.' Nomalanga's voice was deep and sad. '"And I can't see in the dark to catch anything else. So I'll just have to eat you and hope you're too dead to hurt my stomach."

'"No," shouted the Boy. "I'll make you some light to hunt by. Just let me live for a few more minutes."

'King Lion let him go, but he kept a foot on the Boy's foot, in case he ran away. The Boy took out his catapult and a handful of stones. He pulled with all his strength on the catapult and shot a stone high into the black sky. After a second or two, a tiny light appeared in the blackness. The Boy shot another stone and another light appeared.

'He shot more and more stones into the sky and more and more lights appeared. King Lion was very surprised and his laugh was like thunder. "How do you do that?" he cried.

'The Boy said, "It's easy. I just need to shoot hard enough to make holes in the cloth of night. That lets a little of the light of the sun shine through. Is that enough light, King Lion, for you to hunt by?"

'"That will do fine," said King Lion. And he lifted his great foot from the Boy's tiny one, and set off to hunt.

'The Boy was so grateful to be free that he promised to make some more holes the next night. And so he did,' said Nomalanga, blowing her pipe smoke into the night, 'and now there are millions and millions of stars because he worked so hard, such a long, long time ago.'

Chapter 12 *Main Camp*

Next morning, I heard the tourist truck long before I could see it. It sounded out of place in the peace of the morning. Nomalanga had washed my clothes and I had cleaned my trainers the day before. And she'd lent me a razor, so I felt ready (on the outside at least) to meet people again.

The truck arrived and six foreigners got out. They spoke in English and asked Nomalanga questions about living in the wild. They kept saying 'ooh' and 'aah', and wanted to touch everything.

Their guide was called Alfred. After Nomalanga had finished talking to the tourists, she and Alfred had a brief conversation about me. Alfred told me to sit in the front of the truck, beside him.

I didn't know what to say to thank Nomalanga. She had given me a kind of peace, and Sibongile was quieter in my head. So I took both her hands in mine and kissed them.

Then I got into the truck. I turned to wave to Nomalanga. She just stood, shading her eyes, watching us leave, a bright red and yellow cloth wound tightly round her.

When we arrived at Main Camp, I couldn't believe it. It wasn't a camp at all – it was like a village. There were large buildings with grass roofs and open walls under four huge baobab trees. One of the buildings was a restaurant, and I saw gym machines and weights in another room. There were two pale blue swimming pools among flowering bushes, with an artificial waterfall between them. There were chairs with cushions beside the pools. The whole place was high up, looking down on a lake. It was beautiful – and certainly extremely expensive.

Alfred made sure all his tourists were comfortable and then turned to me. 'Let's go,' he said, and I followed him to an office area looking out on to the pools.

There was a fine, but fierce-looking, woman sitting behind a desk.

'This is Tendai, ma'am,' he said. 'Tendai, this is Mrs Ndlovu.'

Mrs Ndlovu stood up. She was tall and the belt and buttons on her smart safari suit shone brightly. 'So . . . you're the runner?' she said, holding out a surprisingly small hand across the desk. I shook it. 'Nomalanga told me about you. All the way from the border.' Her voice sounded like she smoked a lot.

I smiled, but didn't know what to say. I was thinking, 'Could this really be "the boss"?'

'I wanted to ask you if you saw anyone during your trip,' she said. 'We found a dead rhinoceros yesterday. It'd been caught and killed for its horn.'

'That's against the law!' I said.

'Exactly,' she agreed.

'And you think I'm the killer?' The tiniest feeling of anger lit up inside me. It made me feel more like my old self.

'No,' she smiled, and it was like the sun coming out during a storm. 'No, I know it wasn't you. I just wondered if you'd seen anyone out there?'

'You mean the guys who did kill it?' I asked.

'Mm-hmm.' She nodded.

'I wish I had,' I said, 'but I don't remember very much

until about two days ago, when Gogo, er, I mean Nomalanga, found me. I didn't see any people at all till then.'

'Fair enough,' she said. And then, 'Nomalanga said you'd had a bad time. Do you really want to go back?'

I heard Alfred breathe in suddenly behind me. Sibongile was saying, '*We must go back now . . . We need to talk to people and plan things.*'

Until that moment it hadn't occurred to me that I had a choice. I took a slow breath and said, 'Not really. Not yet, no.'

'I have an idea, you see,' Mrs Ndlovu said. 'Have a seat.'

She looked straight at Alfred. 'Thanks, Alfred,' she said. 'You can get some rest now.' Alfred looked at her without smiling or speaking for a couple of seconds. Then he turned and left us. I sat down in a huge, soft armchair.

Mrs Ndlovu opened a small fridge and took out a jug of orange juice. 'You see, Tendai,' she said, 'I need some more help round here. Juice?' I nodded. 'We lost a driver a few days ago. Can you drive?'

'I got my licence last winter,' I told her. 'But I've never driven anything like your safari trucks . . .' The smell of the orange juice brought back memories of the farm where I grew up, and they cut me like a knife.

'Ah, but I need someone to drive me around, not the visitors.' She waved a hand at her legs and I noticed for the first time that the bones of her right leg were bent and her foot was a strange shape.

'Was it a landmine?' I asked before I could stop myself.

'No,' she replied. 'I was born like this.'

Chapter 13 *Driving Mrs Ndlovu*

There was a short pause. I drank some juice. I wasn't sure whether she expected me to go now.

'The landmines near your village,' she said, 'are the first to be found in that area.'

'That's what people are saying,' I answered. 'There's a minefield across the river ...'

'Yes, I know about that.' The clouds were back in her face, and she looked confused and a bit angry. 'And I know a landmine survey was supposed to be done, to check that the area was safe. This was before people first settled in the village.'

'But that's years ago,' I said.

'That's right. But the survey wasn't done then after all, and the present mayor began applying for money for one last year. I wonder ...'

I heard Sibongile's voice, '*And we'll go with Uncle Winston to see the mayor*'.

'Never mind,' said Mrs Ndlovu suddenly. Her smile was back. 'You rest up today, eat plenty, get strong, and tomorrow you can drive me into town. I have things to do there. OK?'

I nodded again. 'Sure,' I said, and finished my juice. Was this too good to be true?

She said, 'Good. Find yourself a room in the staff cottages and get a uniform from the laundry. I'll need you from seven o'clock tomorrow morning.'

That night I watched a little TV, met some of the camp staff and ate well. I saw Alfred briefly, but he didn't speak to me. I collected my uniform and slept in the first comfortable, Western-style bed I'd seen since leaving school.

Sibongile only spoke to me once as I was dropping off to sleep. She said, '*We must do something quickly*.'

'OK,' I said. 'OK, we will.' And I slept without tears.

*   *   *

Mrs Ndlovu's car was a large black Peugeot. She sat beside me in the front. I drove carefully but quite fast along the dirt road until we arrived at the smooth road.

'Now you can really drive,' she said.

I thought, 'She's not so fierce after all.' I settled into my seat and began to have fun.

And so did she. It seemed she liked speed. She sang to the radio and punched my leg in time to the music once or twice. But I could hear Sibongile again, '*We must do something*'. So I said to Mrs Ndlovu, 'About the landmine survey – do you know what the mayor's doing?'

She turned the music down and moved so she could look at me. 'The mayor learned last year about a European organisation, a charity. The charity would provide half the money for the survey and the removal of landmines if he could find the other half.'

'And has he got the money?' I asked.

'He got half from our central government. It helped that his brother works in the Ministry of Home Affairs.'

She was looking at me all the time and I felt a bit embarrassed, but I insisted. 'And the other half, from the charity?'

'It was supposed to arrive a couple of months ago.'

We were coming into the town and I realised with a shock that it was Sikumi, where Amos was in hospital. Tears made it difficult to see, but Mrs Ndlovu's eyes never left my face. I made myself concentrate on her.

'How do you know that?' I asked, taking a quick look at her. She was smiling a little.

'I'm on the town council,' she said. 'I'm the deputy mayor.'

'Wow!' I said. 'Congratulations.'

I managed not to think about how I would feel if I saw Dad or Abigail. I drove slowly, looking for a parking space. Both sides of the road were lined with cars parked side by side, facing the pavement.

Mrs Ndlovu laughed and punched my leg again. 'I got in touch with a small company in Victoria Falls to come and do the survey as soon as the money came through, but I guess it hasn't yet … Park here! At the bank.'

I nosed the car carefully into a space between two trucks. I got out and went round to open the door. Mrs Ndlovu held out a hand and I helped her out without meeting her eyes. She went into the bank. I leant against the Peugeot, trying to decide what to do. Should I ask Mrs Ndlovu if there was time to visit Amos, or should I stay away from everything that reminded me of Sibongile?

The driver of the vehicle next to me leant out of his window. 'Hey, you new?' he asked. He was smoking.

'Yeah,' I said. 'Why? Do you know Mrs Ndlovu?'

'Everyone knows Mrs Ndlovu.' He winked at me, closing his right eye with a knowing smile.

'How often does she come into town?' I asked, ignoring the wink.

'At least once a week. It's usually Alfred who brings her.' He drew slowly on his cigarette, looking questioningly at me.

I wasn't interested in Mrs Ndlovu's relationship with Alfred, so I said, 'Right. See you around,' and I got back into my driving seat. Mrs Ndlovu came out of the bank.

We went to a supermarket. I pushed the shopping trolley and Mrs Ndlovu put sugar, flour and soft drinks into it. I wanted to ask her about talking to the mayor – and about how much she was going to pay me – but this didn't feel like the right moment.

At one point she stood beside a freezer full of meat and looked at me with her head on one side. She said, 'Would you like to eat with me tonight? We could have pepper steak.' Her eyes were very wide and a small smile spread across her lips.

I had the sudden thought, 'She's trying to attract me!' but I didn't really believe it. A powerful woman like that could have anyone she chose.

But later, when we came to pay and I was standing behind her in the queue, she stepped back towards me as if she was going to fall, and leant on my chest. She didn't stand away immediately and her bottom pushed against me. She moved it in a way that I couldn't mistake.

'Wow! She's choosing me!' I thought. I couldn't keep my breathing steady and my heart was beating too fast. I helped her stand away from me again.

Sibongile said, '*Too many people do things because of how they feel rather than what they think.*'

My body wanted me to shout, 'Who cares about thinking!?'

'Thank you,' said Mrs Ndlovu, turning to me with a kind of secret smile. She paid at the checkout and we went to the car.

As we were putting the bags into the boot, Mrs Ndlovu's hand touched mine. She didn't look at me, but she licked her large, soft lips.

Sibongile said, '*You are so sweet, and I think you don't know much about the dirty side of life.*'

My stomach suddenly turned over in horror at myself.

'Mrs Ndlovu, excuse me,' I said, 'but I need the toilet.'

'Fine,' she said, with that smile again. 'I'll wait in the car.'

I walked into the supermarket and along between the shelves towards the back. I found a door that said 'Staff Only'. I pushed through it into the backyard. There were trucks and men working. I walked through the yard and out into the road at the back.

'*What we do with our lives is what we give to ourselves,*' Sibongile said.

I ran.

Chapter 14 *Meeting the mayor*

After wandering the back streets for a while, trying to think, I asked someone the way to the hospital. I soon realised I'd have to walk past the supermarket. I stopped for a minute and looked at all the cars in the car park. The Peugeot was gone. Who had driven it away?

'*You're so sweet,*' Sibongile said. And again I ran, but I could still feel her with me.

When I walked into the hospital waiting room, Abigail's face looked as though she'd seen a ghost. 'Tendai!' she shouted. Other people turned to look at us.

'*Your stepmother is a bit stressed out,*' said Sibongile. I wanted to laugh and cry at the same time. Tears blinded me.

Abigail came up to me and said, 'Oh, Tendai,' very quietly. I thought she would put her arms around me there, in public, but she just took a breath and said, 'Where did you get that uniform?'

'Is everything OK in the village?' I asked. 'How are Memory and Gugu?'

'They're fine,' she said. 'No more landmines so far.'

'Can I see Amos?' I asked.

He was sleeping but looked much stronger. He was in a big room with lots of other patients. When I'd seen that he was OK, Abigail pulled me out of the room and said, 'Come on. Let's get some food and you can tell me where you've been.'

She didn't mention Sibongile, and I couldn't. I just told

her about running across the Wildlife Park for days, and meeting Nomalanga, and that she was a storyteller too. When I told Abigail about driving Mrs Ndlovu, she seemed really pleased, especially when I mentioned her being the deputy mayor.

But when I said I couldn't do what Mrs Ndlovu wanted, she said, 'What do you mean? All you have to do is to tell her that you're not interested in her like that. You're a serious young man with serious ambitions.' Abigail obviously had no idea what it was like being an eighteen-year-old man in the company of a good-looking, inviting woman.

I answered, 'She'd just throw me out anyway. She doesn't need another driver. She has one.'

'Better to have her throw you out, than to be known as someone who runs away all the time!' said Abigail.

My brain just seemed to stop dead.

'You've probably made her angry,' Abigail went on. 'At least you had a job! You'd have been paid, or anyway you'd have had a bed and food. You'd have had something to do to keep your mind busy, to help you get over ...'

My brain had begun to work again. 'I'm sorry, Abigail,' I interrupted. 'Of course, it costs money to feed me. I will look for a job, but it'll have to be one where I don't need to sleep with my boss to keep it!'

'*You're so sweet,*' repeated Sibongile.

'You're so hurt,' said Abigail. 'But at least you haven't done what your father did and "gone away" inside. He'll be very glad to see you back safe.'

I thought, 'I wish he was here. I don't know what I should be doing first – finishing the compound, or finding a job, or trying to get the landmines cleared ...'

Sibongile said, '*Demand that the landmines get cleared!*'

But I said, 'I'll call and leave a message for him at the hotel at Baobab Cross.'

'No need,' Abigail said. 'He's here in town. Uncle Winston thinks he's the best person to persuade the mayor to do something about the landmines. After all, he's Amos's father.'

And at that moment Dad appeared in the doorway of the restaurant. When he saw me, his mouth fell open. Then he ran to us, knocking into a table or two on his way across the room.

I stood up. He came to a stop in front of me and put his hands on my shoulders. He looked deep into my eyes. 'Thank God,' was all he said.

'*Your dad's a good man,*' said Sibongile.

'I ran after you, you know,' Dad said as we sat down, 'But you were right. You can run faster than I can.'

'No comment,' I said with a smile.

He paused, then said, 'Sibongile's buried on the rocky hill.'

I couldn't speak. I didn't want her to be there alone, her body in pieces under the earth. I wanted her to be with me again, watching the sunset. I wanted the whole of the past fortnight to disappear, to un-happen, to leave us in peace. Sibongile said, '*It's not going away...*'

My dad went on, 'After we buried her, we had a meeting. Uncle Winston asked me to represent the village and speak to Mayor Kapuya.'

Abigail said, 'I made an appointment at the Town Hall for us to see him. It's this afternoon.'

Sibongile's voice was there again. '*We'll ask Uncle Winston to help us see the mayor.*'

I asked, 'Could I come with you?'

Dad and Abigail looked at each other. He said, 'As long as you don't get too upset. It'll be difficult for you.'

'I'll be fine,' I said. I'd be doing what Sibongile had wanted to do herself. 'But maybe it's best if we don't tell him my name, in case he's spoken to Mrs Ndlovu,' and I explained what had happened to Dad.

When I finished, all he said was, 'You really loved Sibongile, didn't you?'

'I still do,' I answered.

* * *

Mayor Kapuya was a big man behind a big desk in a big room. He stood up and showed us to some armchairs round a coffee table.

'Mr Muruvi, Mrs Majozi. Come in, come in. You've come about landmines in Mangwe Ford,' he said.

'That's right,' Dad said. 'You must have had Chief Winston Majozi's letter?'

'I did. But tell me again.' He sat down.

Dad took a deep breath. 'Fifteen days ago my son and some other small boys were playing football at the edge of the river-bed. My son was seriously injured by a landmine. He's in hospital now. Eight days later one of the young women working in the vegetable gardens was killed as she bent to pick up what she thought was a big stone. So now we have some questions.'

'Go ahead,' said the mayor, his hands on his large stomach.

'Where have these landmines come from?' asked my dad. 'Why wasn't the survey done that was planned before the village was built? How can the villagers go on living there with this danger hanging over them? And finally, what happened to the money promised for the survey?'

Dad stopped. He was trying not to show his anger.

The mayor said, 'You're right. There should have been a survey years ago. The man who was mayor before me was supposed to arrange it. But it's very expensive. It took me a long time to find a way to get the money, and the costs of the surveying companies keep rising.' He stood up and walked about. 'Our government has promised some, and so has a foreign charity, but no actual money has come through yet.'

This didn't agree with what Mrs Ndlovu had told me. I was about to jump up and say so, when the mayor's secretary brought in tea and biscuits. My dad shook his head at me. The secretary poured the tea.

'Who are these surveyors, anyway?' asked my dad.

The mayor was still walking backwards and forwards on his beautiful carpet.

'The last one to give us a price was Mr Gresham in Victoria Falls,' said the secretary. 'Didn't you . . .?'

The mayor frowned at her and she went out again.

'That's true,' said the mayor. 'They've finished clearing the landmines near Victoria Falls at last. I got in touch with Mr Gresham and a couple of other bigger companies. But they wouldn't agree to start before they'd been paid a large sum of money.'

'Perhaps they've had problems with getting paid in the past?' Dad suggested.

The mayor stood for a moment looking out of the tall window. I wanted to shout at him that he was a liar, but Dad's hand was on my knee, stopping me.

Then Mayor Kapuya turned to us. 'Look,' he said. 'I'm sorry I can't help you just now. But I'll bring this up at the next council meeting and see if we can rearrange our spending.'

Abigail asked, 'When will that be?'

'In about six weeks, I think,' said the mayor. 'It's the Christmas break now, of course.'

'One person a week is being injured or killed now, ' said my father, standing up, his face like stone. 'So that means that a further six people may be injured or die before you can even discuss the matter at a meeting. Is that the best a man in your position can do?' He turned towards the door.

Abigail and I followed. At the door Dad let us pass through and then turned to the mayor. 'Thank you so much for your time, Mr Mayor,' he said in a voice as cold as ice.

I saw the mayor's face, frowning and angry, as the door closed. But he wasn't as angry as I was.

Chapter 15   *What now?*

Dad was angry too. He walked so fast from the Town Hall to the hospital that Abigail and I had to run to keep up. But he went straight to see Amos, who was awake and having a walking lesson. So we didn't discuss the results of the meeting with the mayor until the evening.

By then my anger had cooled a bit, and Dad had become his usual self, calm and decisive.

'You know,' I told him, 'I'm pretty sure the mayor was lying about the money. Mrs Ndlovu said—'

'You may be right, Tendai,' Dad interrupted, 'but there's nothing we can actually do about that at the moment. If the council isn't going to meet for six weeks, then we'll just have to move the whole family into town,' he said.

Abigail took a quick, shocked breath. 'Renting a place in Sikumi would be much too expensive,' she said. 'And we can't stay in town much longer. The church might need our room anytime.'

'If both Tendai and I get jobs . . .' said my dad.

'That's not so easy,' said Abigail. 'I think you were right before. We should finish the compound in the village, so we have somewhere at least we can call home. Then you can start looking for work.'

I suddenly felt bad, so I interrupted. 'I'm sorry I couldn't work with Mrs Ndlovu. She might have been able to help.'

'She still might,' said Dad. 'But it's best not to depend on someone like that. Tomorrow I shall find a way to visit the safari camp, Tendai. I can apologise for your disappearance and see if there's still a job there.'

'I really can't go back, Dad,' I said, panic rising.

'No, not for you. For me,' he answered.

'Ah ha!' I smiled at the thought of Mrs Ndlovu trying her female tricks on my dad. 'Then I wish you luck,' I said.

'After that, I'll go and get Memory and Gugu. Meanwhile, you can start looking for work in town. See if they need anyone at the hospital. If not, keep asking at all the businesses, street by street, until you find something.' Abigail was trying to interrupt him, but he turned to her and looked into her eyes and said, 'I just can't bear to think of Memory and Gugu there, not even for another day.'

Abigail was quiet. I realised how tired they both looked.

I said, 'Would you mind if I stayed with Amos tonight?'

'A very good idea,' said Abigail quickly. 'The house we're staying in is near the church at the end of the street, so you can come and find me if you need to.' She wrote down the address and the phone number.

That reminded me. 'Have you seen Zola, the young woman who gave us the information about artificial legs?' I asked Dad. 'I've lost the list she gave me – or left it in the village.'

'No, I haven't. But someone will know where to find her if you ask.' He and Abigail went in to say goodnight to Amos.

*   *   *

Later, when all was quiet and Amos was sleeping, I sat beside him. I was hearing Sibongile say, '*We must do something quickly*,' over and over again. But I kept seeing my dad's worried face. I felt torn in half, wanting to do as she wanted, but also wanting to help Dad. He hadn't said so, but it was obvious that in fact we had no money at all.

Maybe I slept a little, because suddenly I realised someone else was at Amos's bedside. It was Zola. Her fingernails weren't blue now, they were purple.

'They said you might need another copy of this,' she whispered, and handed me the sheet of paper. She waved a hand towards Amos. 'He's doing very well,' she said.

I smiled at her. 'Yes, he's always been the most cheerful one in the family. He's trying hard with his crutch.'

'He'll be OK,' she said. She sat carefully on the end of the bed and looked at me closely. 'Your mother told me about you, though. I'm glad you came back.'

'So am I,' I said.

'She thinks you need to keep busy,' she said.

'I'll find something. She needn't worry,' I said.

'I work at the local newspaper as a reporter. Shall I keep an eye open for any job advertisements for you?'

'If you want,' I said. 'I'll be looking for myself too.'

'What sort of jobs?' she asked.

'I was going to study sports management, but anything I can get paid for will do for now.'

She stood up. 'Sports …' she said thoughtfully. 'I'll see. Bye for now.' She smiled with a little nod, and left.

I looked at the paper she'd given me. There were two addresses for prostheses, both a long way away, another one for a care home for injured people not far from Bulawayo, and some international addresses for companies that cleared landmines. At the end was Mr Gresham's address in Victoria Falls. I felt my eyes closing as I read, and I slept.

*   *   *

It was midday. The sky was white with the heat. Sibongile was like she used to be, uninjured, wearing a white dress. She was sitting on a large rock and looking down at me. She seemed to be almost part of the sky.

'Don't run away from me this time,' she said.

'I never ran away from you,' I replied, my voice strange and distant.

'You always run away from me these days.' She sounded so sad I began to cry. I said, 'It hurts me so much that I'll never see you again, but your voice is always with me.'

She didn't cry. She said urgently, 'Please don't stop trying to get the landmines cleared.'

'I haven't stopped,' I said. 'But I'll have to work for a bit to help Dad.'

'No. You must clear the Dragons' eggs first. There are many more. But be careful of the mayor.' Her voice was getting further away, although she was still sitting on the rock. 'He is a snake in the grass. Do this for me. Please, Tendai. Then my death will not have been wasted.'

The light was getting stronger and she was disappearing into the whiteness. Her voice was distant, but quite clear. 'For eight days I loved you. Beautiful, beautiful days . . .'

'No!' I cried. 'Don't go . . .'

I woke as I fell off the chair.

Amos moved in his bed. 'Tendai?' he said.

'I'm here,' I replied, as I got up from the floor. My face was wet with tears. 'I never want to let her go,' I said to myself.

Amos was asleep again. I went out to get some air. I needed to think.

Chapter 16 *Decision*

I set off walking along a dark street. As I walked, I thought. Sibongile and Abigail had both said I was in the habit of running away. Looking back, I had to admit that, whenever there was a difficult decision to make, I'd got someone else to make it.

But now if I wanted Sibongile to rest in peace – and to let me have peace – there was something I had to do on my own. I thought, 'The best thing would be to call Victoria Falls from the hospital phone box. But 3 am is not a good time to get a phone call asking for a favour!'

Further on I thought, 'Explaining and getting information on the phone is not the best way. If I'm there, standing in front of him, there's more chance I'll get somewhere.' Sibongile said, '. . . *get people together and demand that the landmines get cleared.*'

I arrived back at the main door to the hospital. I knew that if I stopped now I'd be too afraid to do what I planned. So I walked straight into the hospital, checked on Amos, and told the night nurse that I had to leave. She said she'd keep an eye on him.

I walked out of town on the main road towards Victoria Falls. I knew I had about a thousand kilometres to travel – and I had no idea how I would do it. The moon was a few days off being full and was just setting. I could see lights a long way ahead.

The lights turned out to be at a large petrol station. There was a café with one sleepy girl behind the counter. I looked around for a driver who seemed OK, but there were only a couple of guys there and they looked drunk. I went outside again and sat on the ground by a wall in the dark to wait for dawn.

I couldn't forget Sibongile saying in my dream, '*You always run away from me these days.*' She had never said that when she was alive. In fact, she had never said any of the things she said in my dream when she was alive.

A white man in a clean shirt came out of the men's toilets. He went into the café. When he came out, I went up to him.

'Excuse me, sir,' I said. 'I'm trying to get to Victoria Falls. Could you give me a lift?'

He looked at me, pulled me gently into better light and looked again.

'Why should I do that?' he asked.

I thought for a moment and answered, 'Because it could help a whole village to live without fear. And also because I will tell you stories and keep you entertained on your long journey.'

He laughed. His teeth were white and he didn't smell of drink. 'What's your name?' he asked.

'Tendai Muruvi. Once of the Woods Orange Farm, now of Mangwe Ford.'

'And working as a driver?' He was looking at my uniform.

I answered carefully, 'Er . . . yes. And your name, sir?'

'I'm Don McInley. I run the Miti Miviri Hotel in the town of Victoria Falls.'

'I'm very lucky!' I said. 'And I promise I'll be good company.'

'OK, young Tendai. I'll take you as far as I'm going, as

long as you behave. The minute you give me reason to worry, you're out. Understood?'

We set off in his small truck. The road was mainly straight and it didn't have much traffic, so driving was pretty boring. We passed through one or two small towns and, a bit before midday, through Bulawayo.

At first, I told Mr McInley stories as I'd promised, but later he asked me about the village. I told him about Amos and the landmines. He said he knew Bart Gresham, who lived outside the town at the Falls, near a place called Elephant Junction.

We passed through another town, and he pulled off on to the grass at the side of the road. He took out his cellphone.

He said, 'Now I'll just check Bart is around. He may have gone off on a job … That you, Bart? … I've met a young man who may need your help. Can he find you at home? … Some time tomorrow? … Right, I'll tell him. His name's Tendai … See you, Bart.'

He turned to me and said, 'He'll be in early tomorrow morning, if you can make it before nine.'

'I can try,' I said.

Sibongile said, '*Make plans, talk to people.*'

Then Mr McInley called his wife. 'We'll be having a hungry young visitor this evening,' he told her. I heard her laugh and then ask a question.

'You want to stay the night?' he asked me.

'Oh yes, thank you!' I said. I had no money and had expected to spend the night outside somewhere.

'Right,' he said into the phone. He hung up and said, 'We charge a hundred US dollars a night.'

My mouth was wide open before I realised he was joking, and we both laughed.

'If Bart takes your business he'll owe me a drink,' he said. 'Now tell me another story.'

And he drove on along that long, boring, straight road, with the trees on each side throwing longer and longer shadows in the afternoon sun. My grandmother's stories came back to me, and I told him about clever priests and stupid kings and beautiful young women and talking animals.

Great black clouds came over, but no rain fell on the road. And when we were almost at the end of our journey, I saw a huge white cloud of what looked like steam rising from the ground a few miles ahead.

'That's the Falls,' said Mr McInley. 'You'll hear them from the hotel.'

We arrived at the Miti Miviri Hotel as the sun was getting low. I could smell apple pie and coffee as we went in.

Mr McInley showed me on a map where Bart lived, quite a long way out of the town. He suggested I took a train in the morning. I didn't tell him I had no money.

I ate at a small table on my own in the dining room. There were a few other guests in the hotel, and we all said 'Good evening' to each other. There was a TV lounge, but I found myself falling asleep as I tried to watch TV. So I went off to sleep in my very own hotel room, for the first time in my life.

I could hear the distant thunder of the Falls as I relaxed. I hoped I'd dream of Sibongile again. But all that came into my mind was the angry face of Mayor Kapuya as we left his office.

Chapter 17 *Train trip*

I woke in the dark. I got up, wrote a thank-you note and left as quietly as I could. Outside, in the quiet before dawn, the thunder of the Falls seemed very near.

The hotel wasn't far from the centre of the town. I walked along the road until it crossed the railway, then I followed the rails into the station.

There was a train in the station. People were getting on. I went to join them, but a man in a dark uniform was checking their tickets.

I walked back the way I'd come, along the rails. How was I going to get on to the train?

I could hear the train coming behind me, gathering speed. I stepped to one side as it passed, and began to run along beside it. It was very high off the ground, and I couldn't see anywhere to get up on to it. There were vertical bars beside the doors, but I'd have to jump really high to grab one. I kept running along beside it, telling myself that if Indiana Jones could do it, so could I. Then the train got faster, so I had to jump or give up. I jumped, and managed to pull myself up on to the step, but I didn't try to open the door.

I hung on for what seemed a very long time. The train got faster and faster, and the sun came up. We were out in the land of red earth, small brown trees and an occasional rock.

'Just like the movies,' I thought, feeling really proud of myself. But soon my hands and arms began to hurt. Elephant Junction was a long way out of town.

At last I saw a tiny station ahead, just a platform and a hut, like in a Western film. The train slowed down, but it didn't stop. I saw the name 'Elephant Junction' as it began to pick up speed again, so I jumped off. When I'd rolled over a few times, I stood up and dusted myself off. I walked back to the hut. There was no one there.

A dirt road ran away from the station with a lot of tyre marks on it. I followed it and found a small road turning off, with a postbox on a stick beside it. The name on the box was Gresham. After a while I came to a group of trees.

Under them was a small white house with a bright green roof. Nearby were two long, low buildings. I could hear dogs barking and hoped they were tied up. I'd had one or two bad moments with dogs on the farm when I was little.

I went up to the front door and knocked.

A blonde woman carrying a small boy on her hip opened the door. She looked surprised to see me.

'Oh! I wasn't expecting anyone. What did you want?'

'I'd like to speak to your husband if he's Bart Gresham, please,' I said. Her eyes were bluer than the sky.

'I see. He's out with the dogs at the moment and then he has to leave. Could you come back tomorrow?'

'I'm sorry to bother you, ma'am,' I said, 'but I do need to speak to him urgently. Mr McInley checked with him yesterday that it would be OK. My name's Tendai. I won't keep him long.'

'What's it about?' she asked. The little boy reached out a hand towards me.

'I can't touch you, little one,' I said. 'I'm covered in dust.'

'This is Gareth,' she said, and smiled, waiting for me to explain my business.

I said, 'I wanted to ask your husband's advice about clearing landmines in the village where I ... where I live now.' For the first time for days, Sibongile's head in the grass had come into my mind and I couldn't breathe.

Mrs Gresham looked me right in the eyes for a long moment. 'He won't be long,' she said. 'Would you like to sit there in the shade? I'll bring you some lemonade.'

Bart Gresham came round the side of the house a few minutes later. He sat down opposite me at the table under the tree. He was tall, blond and suntanned. He didn't smile.

'You need some advice about clearing landmines?' he said.

'Yes. Our village is Mangwe Ford, near the border with Mozambique. There was going to be a survey, but the money hasn't come yet. Seventeen days ago, my little brother lost his right hand and part of his left leg. And ... then ...' I looked down at my hands on the table.

Mrs Gresham had come out with the lemonade.

'Someone else was hurt?' she asked gently.

'My girlfriend,' I said. I swallowed, and my voice sounded strange when I said, 'She was killed.'

'Right,' Bart Gresham said. 'And this is by the ford?'

I took a deep breath. 'Yes, and in the river-bed. Some people think some landmines from a minefield across the river moved with the floods. But others think ...'

'That's not likely,' Mr Gresham said. 'As it's a ford and there's a road that crosses the river, it's possible that a group of soldiers or revolutionaries set the landmines to catch a particular enemy. They probably didn't have time to mark the place properly. Even if there was a map, it'll be lost now, especially if they were beaten or killed.'

'You know the place, then?' I asked.

'The mayor of Sikumi's office wrote to me some time ago asking for a price to do a survey there. I had a look at the maps.'

'And decided not to do it?' I spoke almost rudely.

'Tendai,' he said seriously, 'the town council hasn't come up with the money. I've done too many surveys without being paid – I have to make a living.' He waved a hand at his wife and the house.

'I know,' I said, trying to relax. 'And perhaps it didn't seem urgent then, or even necessary. But now someone has died and no one can live there without fear.'

'Even to go and have a look ...' His cellphone rang. 'Excuse me, Tendai. I've been expecting this call.' He stood up and walked into the sunlight.

Sibongile said, '*We can put out a message on the Internet, asking for money and help*.'

Mr Gresham soon came back. 'I'll have to ask you to wait a few days, Tendai, I'm afraid,' he said. 'My brother needs my help, and anyway I need some time to check the letters and documents I've got about your village first.'

Sibongile said, '*But be careful of the mayor*.'

I said, 'Every day we leave it may mean another injury or death. Please come as soon as you can. I'll find some money. I'll do whatever it takes.'

Mrs Gresham put a hand on her husband's arm. 'Surely your brother can wait?' she said quietly.

'How did you get here?' Mr Gresham asked me.

'On the train,' I said.

He almost smiled. 'You jumped off? Rather you than me.'

Mrs Gresham said, 'Come in and have some breakfast.'

Chapter 18 *At Victoria Falls*

After a wash, and with a large breakfast inside us, Mr Gresham said to me, 'Have you seen the Falls?'

'No, sir. Only in photos,' I answered.

'Then you should go with my wife and son this morning,' he said. 'I have to check out some things before I'll know if I can help you, Tendai.'

'That'll be wonderful,' said Mrs Gresham.

Mr Gresham smiled. 'But be careful. It can be quite dangerous.' He reached out a hand and laid it on Mrs Gresham's stomach. I realised she was pregnant.

'We'll take care, won't we, Tendai?' She laughed.

'If we set off before dawn tomorrow,' Mr Gresham said to me, 'could we make it to the village before dark?'

I tried not to smile too much. 'To Sikumi, yes,' I answered. 'There's nowhere to stay in the village.'

'I'll see how things go this morning,' he said, and stood up.

* * *

Mrs Gresham and little Gareth and I set off for the Falls in a tiny, bright red truck. It was old and made various noises that would have interested my dad.

Driving up to the entrance to the Falls, we could see the spray from the falling water rolling and rising like living clouds in the air.

We went through the gate and walked along the smooth tourist path through the rainforest, the thundering sound getting louder and louder. There were monkeys in the trees and wild pigs in the grass. Now and again the gentle wind brought some of the spray down on us like rain, but we still couldn't see the falling water.

Mrs Gresham pushed Gareth's pushchair and I walked beside her, ready to stop him if he tried to climb out. But he was too scared of the noise.

It was deafening, and the ground was shaking. Suddenly, between the trees, we could look along a huge cut in the earth. Vertical walls faced each other. Over the left-hand wall the river poured in great brown and white curtains, their bottoms lost in the boiling mists below. In the sunshine above, the spray made rainbows, one above the other up into the sky.

'Mummy,' Gareth said, his little face changing as he began to cry. 'Too big!'

We turned back into the forest along the main path. Mrs Gresham picked Gareth up and held him tight. He calmed down quickly and began laughing at the monkeys. She put him back in the pushchair.

We turned left along a short path and came out facing the Falls, across the great cut. It was breathtaking – such power, so much water, so many rainbows. I could feel the thunder in my bones. Now I understood why our traditions told of the huge powers of the River God. What stories I could make from this!

Gareth enjoyed it this time, especially the spray falling like rain. We got very wet and ran away laughing.

* * *

As we drove up to the little house with the green roof, Mr Gresham came out. He had some files under his arm, which he began laying out on the table under the tree.

'Look at this, Tendai,' he said, calling me over to see.

Mrs Gresham lifted a hand to us and took Gareth indoors.

Mr Gresham smiled at her, but turned to me. 'I had the mayor's office send me copies of these documents when they wanted me to give them a price to do the survey,' he explained. 'The first letters are from years ago, before they built the village at the ford. Then a year ago there was this letter from the European Organisation Against Landmines.'

'What does it say?' I asked, hearing Sibongile's voice in my head again. *'We need to talk to people and plan things.'*

'Basically it's to say that when the government in Harare gives a certain sum of money to the town council in Sikumi, the Europeans will give the same amount.'

'And have they done that?' I asked, longing to squeeze Sibongile's hand in mine.

'There's a copy of a document here that shows that the money from the government was paid over to Mayor Kapuya in June this year.'

'That's six months ago,' I said. 'And he told us there wasn't any money at all. So he was lying!'

'It seems so,' said Mr Gresham, picking up another paper. 'Here's a letter to me signed by a Mrs Ndlovu that agrees to my price if the money arrives from the Europeans before the rains come.'

'Which should have come in November,' I said.

'But I haven't heard anything else,' Mr Gresham said, collecting the papers into the files.

'And now it's December,' I said. 'No money ...'

'And hardly any rain,' Mr Gresham added. 'If it stays dry, we could start a survey – if there was money.'

My heart beat faster. He was taking this seriously. He really might do something about it – if the mayor paid him.

'So I called your Town Hall,' he went on. 'And I got the mayor's secretary.'

'What did she say?' I asked, remembering that she was the first person to mention 'Mr Gresham in Victoria Falls'.

'At first she agreed there'd been money from Harare. But then she wasn't very clear about what had happened with the Europeans. I had the feeling that she was hiding something.'

'But be careful of the mayor. He's a snake in the grass,' repeated Sibongile from my dream.

'She seemed frightened of Mr Kapuya when I was in his office with my parents,' I said.

'So we'd better go and see what's happening,' said Mr Gresham. He led me into the house. 'How were the Falls?'

*   *   *

Next morning it was still dark when I whispered goodbye and thank you to Mrs Gresham. I went out to get into Bart Gresham's pick-up truck. It was white, with four doors and a short, thick radio aerial on the front.

And there was a huge black dog sitting by the passenger door. It yawned at me, reminding me of crocodiles. My heart thundered like the Falls and I couldn't move. I told myself, 'You've slept in trees with monkeys and walked with lions and elephants. You can't be afraid of a pet dog!'

Mr Gresham came out of the house with a travel bag. He looked at the dog, and he looked at me. He said, 'He's quite safe if I'm around. Kit, come and meet Tendai.'

The dog came to me and sat at my feet. His head was on a level with my waist. He lifted a foot and held it up to me. 'Shake hands and say hello,' Mr Gresham said to me.

I did as I was told. 'Hello, er … Kit.' Kit's foot was warm and hard and filled my hand completely.

Kit looked me right in the eyes for a second and then gently took his foot away and walked back to the truck.

'He usually travels beside me,' Mr Gresham said. 'But I think he'll be happier in the back today. He can be jealous.'

I thought, 'Ah. "One who loves by holding on."' We got in and drove quietly away in the dark before dawn.

Chapter 19　*On the road*

The sun quickly lifted to the north and we sped along the almost empty road, through the dry lands and later the forests.

We talked about our different schools and my never-to-happen degree. Mr Gresham seemed to understand my disappointment. We told each other stories about when we were kids and I mentioned my interest in traditional stories. I also told him that I'd met Mrs Ndlovu and that she was the deputy mayor.

He made a call to his wife about two hours out and then he asked me, 'Was your girlfriend called Sibongile?'

'Yes,' I answered. 'Was I talking in my sleep?'

'And your brother is Amos?' he went on.

'I'm sorry,' I said, turning to him. 'I'm sorry if I woke you.'

'It reminded me of …' But he stopped speaking, his face suddenly looking young and lost. There was a silence.

'I … think it's getting better,' I said at last. 'At least when I'm awake it's better. I don't feel like crying so much now. I do hear her voice, but it doesn't make me as sad as it did.'

'You're keeping your mind on the future?' he asked.

'Yeah, I guess so,' I said. 'There are things I must do, so I think about them.' I didn't mention how my anger often helped to crowd out my sadness.

'Always look forward,' he said. 'If you think about the past, you'll feel you could have changed things.'

His voice was very hard. I asked, 'What happened?'

'My brother was killed.' He spoke from far away. 'I saw it.'

Horrified, I thought of Amos. 'How?' I asked. 'Where?'

'He was pulled from our boat by a crocodile,' he said. 'I just sat in the boat and screamed. I was too young to know that you can choose what to think about when you're awake, even if you can't when you're asleep.' He turned to me with a small smile. 'So tell me a traditional story,' he said.

'Are you interested in that kind of thing?' I asked.

'Tell me one, and I'll let you know,' he answered.

So I told him my story of the Dragons' eggs.

He was quiet when I finished. Then he said, 'Dragons' eggs … That's a good way to get the kids to listen. Any more?'

'Sure,' I said. 'Now?'

'Now,' he replied, his eyes on the long straight road.

'This one came to me last night,' I said. 'Long ago, there was a Young King from the south, visiting the Old King of the Land of the Falls. When the time came to go, the Old King asked the Young King, "What will your leaving present be?"

'The Young King wanted to prove he was cleverer than the Old King. "I'd like one of your rainbows," he said. "You have many more in your country than I do in mine."

'The Old King smiled and said, "Rainbows can't be caught, but I'll give you a living rainbow." And the next day, when the Young King was leaving, the Old King gave him a bird that was blue and green and purple and gold. The Young King thought the Old King was being stupid, but he pretended to be grateful and took the rainbow-coloured bird back to his country, where he gave it to his youngest and prettiest Wife.

'His Wife was sorry for it. It wouldn't eat or drink and just sat in its box, waiting to die. She begged the Young King to let it go, and in the end he agreed. It flew high into the sky, calling out its happiness. Then it fell downwards, rolling over and over, its colours shining in the sun. Just before it hit the ground, it flew up again. It did this many times, and then it flew away. The Wife clapped her hands and laughed and the Young King was glad to see his pretty wife so happy.

'It was their habit to sit together on the rocks above his compound each evening, watching the sun go down. One evening they heard a strange cry, and a rainbow bird came falling out of the sky towards them. It settled on a rock nearby, its head on one side, looking at them.

'Suddenly, another rainbow bird arrived, and then another, and another. Soon the Young King and his Wife were sitting on a hill covered in rainbows. "The Old King is not so stupid, after all," thought the Young King, but his Wife only saw the beauty all around her.'

Mr Gresham looked at me briefly. 'Can't clap when I'm driving,' he said.

'*It seems right to tell stories,*' said Sibongile.

* * *

We got into town just after sunset with the full moon rising. At the house by the church, Dad opened the door.

'So,' he said, his eyes shining. 'You ran off again, but you've brought someone back. Come in, come in.'

'Dad,' I said, 'this is Bart Gresham, from Vic Falls. He has some news for you. Mr Gresham, my dad, Shamba Muruvi.'

They shook hands and we sat down round the kitchen table.

'Abigail and the girls are at the hospital,' said Dad. 'Victoria Falls, eh? Been driving all day? Tea? Coffee?'

'That's right,' said Mr Gresham. 'Nothing, thanks. My news is that the town council of Sikumi asked me to give them a price for doing a survey of Mangwe Ford last year. I have copies of letters showing that there was money from Harare and more expected from a charity.'

'So the mayor was lying,' said my father.

'It seems he was.' Mr Gresham smiled. 'Perhaps we should go and ask him what has happened to the money?'

Sibongile's warning rang in my head. '*He's a snake in the grass.*' I said, 'I think you should be careful. If the mayor has been stealing council money ...'

'You're right, Tendai,' said Mr Gresham. 'We should have a plan in case there's trouble.'

My dad looked from one to the other of us. 'Some kind of insurance?'

Mr Gresham had brought his file in and was laying out the papers on the table. 'We could make copies of the most important letters ...' he said.

'And,' I interrupted, 'give them to Zola. She works at the newspaper.'

'Zola?' my father questioned.

'You know – the volunteer at the hospital who gave us the list with Mr Gresham's name on,' I explained.

'That's a good idea,' said Dad. 'But there's someone else who might help too, and I went to see her the day you left.'

I knew he meant Mrs Ndlovu, but I pretended I didn't.

Mr Gresham raised a questioning eyebrow.

My dad went on, 'I got a lift out to your safari camp, Tendai, and asked for Mrs Ndlovu.' His eyes were laughing but his face was very serious. 'She agreed to see me and we had ... a discussion.'

'I'm glad I wasn't there,' I said, feeling very shy in front of Mr Gresham, who was listening carefully.

'Yes. It was better you weren't!' Dad said, trying hard not to smile. 'In the end she agreed she shouldn't have been so inviting, but she said it was your fault for being so attractive!'

I had to laugh. 'Did she do the same to you?' I asked Dad. I saw understanding appear in Mr Gresham's face.

'No, of course not,' Dad said. 'But she did offer me a job for two days a week as a mechanic!'

'Cool!' I said. 'Did you accept?'

'Of course. I start the day after tomorrow. But that's by the way. The important thing is that I told her about our interview with the mayor. She said that the last time she looked at the town council accounts, there was no record of either the Harare money or the charity money. But she agreed that the decision to do the survey had been made months ago and said she'd check again.'

'So the only reason I haven't been asked to start yet is because the money is missing,' Mr Gresham said.

Chapter 20 *Night hunt*

Dad stood up. 'That's right. So we'll need to visit the Town Hall first thing in the morning...'

The telephone in the hall rang while Dad was speaking. He went to answer it.

When Dad came back into the kitchen, his eyes were wide open and he was almost dancing with impatience.

'That was Mrs Ndlovu,' he said. 'She's at the police station. She says she thinks she's got proof that the mayor put the survey money into his own bank account. And now he seems to have made a run for it. The police were following him...'

'Were? Did they lose him?' asked Mr Gresham.

'Yes. Their car has broken down,' said Dad.

'So where's the mayor now?' asked Mr Gresham.

Dad said in an unbelieving voice, 'It seems he's driving along the dirt road to Mangwe Ford!'

'Why on earth?' Mr Gresham looked surprised. Then he said, 'Of course! It crosses the river and then the border into Mozambique. And there are no border police there. Come on! Let's try and catch our friend, Mayor Kapuya.'

We all three ran out to his truck.

'Stay there, Kit!' Mr Gresham called to the dog in the back as we jumped into the front seats. 'It'll be an uncomfortable ride.'

As we sped along the road in the dark towards Baobab Cross, Bart Gresham spoke on the radio and finally got in touch with the police in the broken-down police car. They were only a hundred metres or so along the dirt road.

'Try and get your car off the road so we can get past,' he said to them. 'Can one of you come with us?' They agreed that we'd stop for the inspector, and signed off.

Dad turned to Bart Gresham. 'Mr Gresham . . .

'Call me Bart, please,' he said, eyes on the road.

'Right. And I'm Shamba,' my dad said. 'Well, Bart, it seems the mayor caught Mrs Ndlovu checking the files about the money and locked her in an empty office. I'm not sure if he'll have a gun, but he'll certainly be desperate.'

'How did she get out?' I asked Dad.

Dad laughed. 'Well, luckily, she had her cellphone, and called Alfred.'

Just then I saw the light at the Baobab Cross Hotel. 'Turn here!' I shouted to Bart.

Bart turned off on to the dirt road far too fast, raising a huge cloud of dust in the light of the full moon.

We soon found the police car, its lights out, but white against the dark trees. Bart stopped and a man ran forward. He jumped in behind me and we raced away.

'Inspector Ncube,' said the man, and we all tried to shake hands. But the truck was behaving like a wild horse and we had to hold on tight. I couldn't believe the treatment Bart was giving it, and I wondered how Kit was.

Bart seemed to know what I was thinking. 'Kit will be fine,' he said to me with a laugh. He was enjoying himself, in spite of having spent all day driving. 'And so will the truck. It's a good thing we filled up with petrol in Bulawayo,' he added.

We came to the top of the rise. In the moonlight, we could see the road running down to the forest and the wide river-bed. About halfway down we could see headlights shining up into the sky.

'He's come off the road!' shouted my dad.

'Get ready!' said Inspector Ncube. 'He may have others with him.'

'I'll pull up near him,' said Bart. 'If you get out of the passenger doors really quietly, you can take him by surprise.'

'All of you, stay with your vehicle, please,' said the inspector. 'He may have a gun.'

We pulled up near where the mayor's dark truck had come off the road. The front wheels were resting on a large rock and its lights were shining crazily at the tops of the trees. There was no sign of anybody.

The inspector climbed out quietly. No gunfire.

Bart got out too. 'My dog can follow him by his smell,' he whispered to the inspector. 'Kit! Come!' And he, Kit and the inspector went carefully down to the mayor's truck.

We watched as Kit put his face into the driver's seat. Then he set off into the bushes, following the mayor's smell. A few moments later there was a scream of fear, and Bart stepped on to the road and called us. We ran down to find Mayor Kapuya lying under a tree. Kit was standing on his chest and the inspector was telling him he was under arrest.

*   *   *

It took until midnight to get the mayor to the police station in Sikumi and the witness statements made. As we were finishing, Zola arrived.

'I'm here as a reporter this time,' she said with a smile. Her nails were now green with white stripes. 'My article about this will be on the front page of tomorrow's paper.'

Chapter 21 *Mrs Ndlovu takes over*

Next morning, Bart spread out the newspaper on the coffee table in the lounge of the hotel where he was staying. Dad and I leaned forward in our armchairs to read.

There was a huge headline on the front page followed by Zola's article.

MAYOR KAPUYA UNDER ARREST

Mayor Method Kapuya was arrested after an exciting car chase involving a police car and a private vehicle last night. He was on his way to the Mozambique border crossing beyond Mangwe Ford.

He had tried to leave the country because a large sum of money is missing from the town council accounts.

This money was given by central government to pay for the landmine survey of the area around Mangwe Ford, where one person has been injured and another killed in the last three weeks.

Mr Bart Gresham, a landmine expert from Victoria Falls, and his dog, Kit, were involved in the chase. The arresting officer was Inspector Ncube, and Shamba and Tendai Muruvi of Mangwe Ford were also present.

The police are now investigating Mayor Kapuya's personal bank accounts.

'So what happens now?' I asked.

'Now,' said a lazy voice behind me, 'I move into the mayor's office and try and sort things out.'

Mrs Ndlovu and Alfred were standing behind me.

I jumped up and said determinedly, 'Good morning, Mrs Ndlovu.' I nodded to Alfred. He smiled a one-sided smile.

'And you, Shamba,' she went on, as my dad and Bart stood up too, 'can go back with Alfred to the camp and keep it going for me. Tendai, you owe me that uniform!'

Bart held out his hand to her. 'Bart Gresham, Mrs Ndlovu. From Vic Falls. We've written to each other. If you're ready to make a deal with me, I'll get straight on and start surveying the village for any other unexploded landmines.'

Mrs Ndlovu took a deep breath and pulled herself up to her full height as she shook his hand. She smiled her special smile at this tall, handsome man.

'I'm ready to make a deal with you any day,' she said. 'It's very good to meet you at last.' She moved to an armchair and sat down, crossing her legs to hide the bad one. Dad looked at me and raised an eyebrow.

Mrs Ndlovu continued, 'How about a small amount now for expenses and the main fee in three months when we've got some money back from Kapuya's account?'

'Not perfect,' answered Bart as he sat down again, 'but possible. And it would help if we could move the people out altogether for a while. Any idea where they could go?'

'But there must be fifteen or more families,' said my dad.

Mrs Ndlovu looked up at Alfred. 'Would they be able to stay in the old safari camp, Alfred?' she asked.

'The huts aren't really waterproof any more,' Alfred answered, 'but as long as it doesn't rain they'd be fine.'

'I'll send a note to Chief Winston Majozi and suggest it,' she said. 'It seems then, Bart, that you could start very soon.'

'Yes, it does, ma'am,' said Bart. 'We'd better get out there today and have a look.' He stood up.

Sibongile said, '*We'll make sure everyone hears about Amos, and the danger we live in.*'

I said, 'Shall we ask Zola from the newspaper if she'd like to come along? She may want to do a follow-up on her story.'

* * *

We picked Abigail and Amos up at the hospital. The doctors thought it would be good for Amos to have 'a breath of fresh air'. So, when we set off for the village that afternoon, he and Dad and Abigail sat in the front of Bart's truck, and Kit, Zola and I sat in the back. Kit lay full length on the floor, his paw on my foot, reminding me of the lion in Nomalanga's story. Bart drove more slowly this time.

When we got to the village, Dad went to see Uncle Winston and they called a meeting to introduce Bart. Kit stayed in the truck, lying down in the back.

Zola asked me to show her the place where Amos was hurt. She took a photograph of the river-bed.

'Now, will you show me where Sibongile was killed?' she asked me quietly.

I couldn't speak, but I took her to where work on the new garden had stopped. Zola walked out towards the hole in the ground, very carefully.

I wanted to hold her back, but I couldn't move.

Then I heard Sibongile's voice. '*She's dead now.*'

'Zola!' I called in panic. 'Please don't go there!'

Zola took another photo and came back towards me. 'I just needed to see the place, so I can write about it,' she said.

Chapter 22   *Goodbye*

When Zola and I got back to the clearing by the road, people were gathering to meet Bart. We sat on the ground among them.

'Do you remember,' Zola asked quietly, 'I said I'd look at the job advertisements for you?'

'Yeah,' I said, glad to have something else to talk about. Seeing that hole in the ground had brought it all back.

'Well, there's a job going at the care home for people hurt by landmines near Bulawayo. I visit there as a volunteer too. And Amos will be going there for a few weeks soon. It's called Lazarus Lodge.'

'What sort of job?' I asked.

'They need someone to help organise sports and games.'

'For people with no legs?' I asked.

'Well, most of them have at least one leg,' she answered with a laugh.

'I'm sorry,' I said, feeling really stupid. 'I didn't think. It's just ... strange ... to think of teams of injured children playing football or basketball, or whatever.'

'They're good. And sport is very important to them – like it is to you and me. Will you come and visit them with me tomorrow?'

I looked at little Amos, sitting in a circle of his friends, who were all admiring his crutch and touching his handless arm.

'*You know,*' said Sibongile, '*we could do something . . .*'

'Yes,' I answered Zola. 'I'd like that.'

Uncle Winston had explained to everyone in the village that they must all pack enough things to last them a month and leave the next day for the old safari camp. Now he introduced Bart, who stood up to speak.

'Good afternoon, everyone,' Bart said. 'I just want you to know what I'm going to do and why it's best if no one is here while I do it.'

Some people clapped.

'But first I have to introduce you to my expert landmine finder. His name is Kit. You may think he looks a bit unfriendly, but I promise that, if he's with me, he's the kindest gentleman on earth.'

All the villagers looked at each other in confusion.

Bart called out, 'Kit!' and Kit jumped out of the truck and ran up to Bart. He stood beside him, completely still.

'Ah, ah,' people said. One or two gave a little scream.

'I will mark out the ground in large squares, and Kit will go into each square and smell for landmines. If he finds one, we'll mark where it is for the explosive experts to come and explode it. Then we'll go on looking.'

The sun had started to go down. The sky was turning yellow. Bart went on, 'I think there are two kinds of landmine here – large ones to destroy vehicles by the road to the ford, and smaller ones to injure people beside the river.'

I smiled at Zola and stood up.

'I won't be long,' I said.

She nodded and went on making notes from what Bart was saying.

I walked away from the meeting and up to the rocky hill

where Sibongile and I had talked and kissed that evening a lifetime ago.

As I walked, I realised I couldn't have come back until I'd done as she wanted and made sure the landmines would be cleared. Now that was happening, I knew I had to find the strength to face life without her, to admit to myself that she was really gone.

I climbed slowly up to the rocks. There was a flat, smooth stone, shining pink in the late sun, near the top of the hill. On it the words 'Sibongile, gone too soon' were written in gold. A gentle wind touched the dead flowers someone had laid on it.

I sat there, beside Sibongile, and didn't try to stop the tears.

I heard her say, '*What we do with our lives is what we give to ourselves.*' I said her name over and over again.

The sun had almost gone when I finally looked up at it. I could hear singing and music down in the village. It was a day for celebration.

With tears drying on my face, I whispered, 'Your life, and your death, have not been wasted, Sibongile. I'll try to let go of you now, but I will never stop hating the landmine that killed you. I will always miss you, and I'll never forget your wisdom, and your beauty, and our eight wonderful days.'

'Beautiful, beautiful days,' whispered the wind, but Sibongile's voice was silent.

I turned away from the grave and walked slowly down the hill.